EDITOR: Maryanne Blacker
DESIGN DIRECTOR: Neil Carlyle
FOOD EDITOR: Pamela Clark

• • •

DESIGNERS: Christie & Eckermann

• • •

DEPUTY FOOD EDITOR: Barbara Northwood
ASSISTANT FOOD EDITORS: Jan Castorina,
Karen Green
ASSOCIATE FOOD EDITOR:
Enid Morrison
CHIEF HOME ECONOMIST: Kathy Wharton
HOME ECONOMISTS: Jon Allen, Jane Ash,
Tikki Durrant, Sue Hipwell, Karen Hughes,
Karen Maughan, Voula Mantzouridis, Louise Patniotis
EDITORIAL COORDINATOR: Elizabeth Hooper
KITCHEN ASSISTANT: Amy Wong

• • •

STYLISTS: Rosemary de Santis,
Carolyn Fienberg, Michelle Gorry,, Jacqui Hing,
Victoria Lewis, Anna Phillips
PHOTOGRAPHERS: Kevin Brown, Robert Clark,
Andre Martin, Robert Taylor, Jon Waddy

• • •

HOME LIBRARY STAFF:
ASSISTANT EDITOR: Judy Newman
DESIGNER: Paula Wooller
EDITORIAL COORDINATOR: Lara Quinlin

• • •

ACP PUBLISHER: Richard Walsh
ACP ASSOCIATE PUBLISHER: Bob Neil

• • •

Produced by The Australian Women's Weekly Home Library.
Typeset by Photoset Computer Service Pty Ltd, and Letter
Perfect, Sydney. Printed by Dai Nippon Co., Ltd in Japan.
Published by Australian Consolidated Press,
54 Park Street Sydney.
♦ AUSTRALIA: Distributed by Network Distribution Company,
54 Park Street Sydney, (02) 282 8777.
♦ UNITED KINGDOM: Distributed in the U.K. by Australian
Consolidated Press (UK) Ltd, 20 Galowhill Rd, Brackmills,
Northampton NN4 OEE (0604) 760 456.
♦ CANADA: Distributed in Canada by Whitecap
Books Ltd, 1086 West 3rd St,
North Vancouver V7P 3J6 (604) 980 9852.
♦ NEW ZEALAND: Distributed in New Zealand by Netlink
Distribution Company, 17B Hargreaves St, Level 5,
College Hill, Auckland 1 (9) 302 7616.
♦ SOUTH AFRICA: Distributed in South Africa by Intermag,
PO Box 57394, Springfield 2137 (011) 493 3200.
ACN 000 031 747.

• • •

Delicious Desserts
Includes index.
ISBN 0 947128 94 5

1. Desserts. (Series: Australian Women's
Weekly Home Library).
641.86

• • •

© ACP 1992 (Reprint)
This publication is copyright. No part of it may be reproduced
or transmitted in any form without the written permission
of the publishers.

• • •

COVER: Chocolate Mallow Roll with Raspberry
Sauce, page 67.
Plates & glass: Limoges; fabric: J.D.K. & J.M. Imports Pty Ltd.
OPPOSITE: From top: Apricot Almond Pithivier; Gateau
Saint Honore with Raspberry Cream, page 82.
BACK COVER: Clockwise from back left: Chantilly Berry
Parfait, page 2, Fresh Tangerine Jelly, page 4,
Meringue Kisses with Passionfruit Glaze, page 48.

This is unashamedly a book of temptations! In it, you will find desserts for entertaining in style, as well as treats for your family. Testing and tasting recipes for our cookbooks is always fun (and yes, hard work), but few books have been as delightful to produce as this one. Whether it's a classic self-saucing pud, a cool and classy sorbet terrine or a pretty meringue and ice-cream swan, each recipe is a taste sensation. We hope you enjoy them as much as we did.

Pamela Clark
FOOD EDITOR

BRITISH & NORTH AMERICAN READERS: Please note that Australian cup and spoon measurements are metric. Conversion charts for cup and spoon measurements and oven temperatures appear on page 126. A glossary explaining unfamiliar terms and ingredients appears on page 125.

ISLAND FRUITS WITH LIQUEUR CREAM

Crème de Menthe is a mint-flavoured liqueur. Dessert is best made on day of serving; keep, covered, in refrigerator. Recipe unsuitable to freeze.

565g can longans, drained
565g can seedless jackfruit, drained
2 medium bananas, chopped
1 small papaw, chopped
1 small pineapple, chopped
4 banana passionfruit
LIQUEUR CREAM
300g carton sour cream
¼ cup honey
2 tablespoons Crème de Menthe
green food colouring

Combine all fruit in large bowl; mix well. Place a heaped tablespoon of liqueur cream into 8 glasses (1 cup capacity). Add fruit, top with remaining cream. Refrigerate before serving.
Liqueur Cream: Combine all the ingredients in small bowl.
Serves 8.

CHANTILLY BERRY PARFAITS

Cointreau is an orange-flavoured liqueur. Use any combination of fresh or frozen berries for this recipe. Parfaits are best made close to serving time. This recipe is not suitable to freeze or microwave.

¼ cup flaked almonds
½ cup water
¼ cup castor sugar
500g fresh or frozen berries
300ml carton thickened cream
2 tablespoons sour cream
¼ cup icing sugar
2 tablespoons Cointreau

Toast almonds on oven tray in moderate oven for about 5 minutes.
Combine water and castor sugar in small saucepan, stir over heat, without boiling, until sugar is dissolved, bring to boil, reduce heat, simmer, uncovered, without stirring, for about 5 minutes or until liquid is reduced by half. Pour hot sugar syrup over berries in heatproof bowl; cool to room temperature.
Beat creams, sifted icing sugar and liqueur in small bowl with electric mixer until firm peaks form. Layer berry mixture and cream mixture in 4 glasses (1 cup capacity). Sprinkle with almonds.
Serves 4.

PEACHY CHAMPAGNE JELLY

We used Seagram's Peach Liqueur in this recipe. Jelly can be made a day ahead; keep, covered, in refrigerator. This recipe is not suitable to freeze.

1 tablespoon gelatine
¼ cup water
⅓ cup castor sugar
¾ cup peach nectar
1½ cups champagne
2 tablespoons peach liqueur

Sprinkle gelatine over water in small bowl, stand in small pan of simmering water, stir until dissolved (or microwave on HIGH for about 30 seconds). Combine gelatine mixture, sugar and nectar in small saucepan, stir over heat, without boiling, until sugar is dissolved. Remove from heat, cool 5 minutes; stir in champagne and liqueur. Allow bubbles to subside, pour mixture into 4 glasses (¾ cup capacity), refrigerate until set. Serve with extra cream and fruit, if desired.
 Serves 4.

LEFT: From left: Island Fruits with Liqueur Cream, Chantilly Berry Parfaits, Peachy Champagne Jelly.

Glasses from Village Living; tiles from Northbridge Ceramic & Marble Centre

FRESH TANGERINE JELLY

Grand Marnier is an orange-flavoured liqueur. Jelly can be made a day ahead; keep, covered, in refrigerator. This recipe is not suitable to freeze.

**6 medium tangerines
1 tablespoon Grand Marnier
1 cup water
½ cup castor sugar
2 tablespoons gelatine
½ cup water, extra**

Lightly oil 4 moulds (1 cup capacity). Blend or process tangerines until smooth, strain juice into large bowl, discard pulp (you will need 2½ cups juice); stir in liqueur. Combine water and sugar in small saucepan, stir over heat, without boiling, until sugar is dissolved; remove from heat.
  Sprinkle gelatine over extra water in small bowl, stand in small pan of simmering water, stir until dissolved (or microwave on HIGH for about 40 seconds); cool 5 minutes. Stir gelatine mixture and sugar syrup into juice mixture. Pour into prepared moulds, refrigerate until set.
  Serves 4.

DOUBLE CHOCOLATE SNOWBALLS

Crème de Cacao is a chocolate-flavoured liqueur. You will need about 8 passionfruit for this recipe. Sauce and cakes can be made 2 days ahead; keep, covered, in refrigerator. Uniced cakes can be frozen for 3 months. Recipe not suitable to microwave.

**90g unsalted butter
1 tablespoon raspberry jam
¼ cup castor sugar
3 eggs, separated
100g dark chocolate, melted
½ cup packaged ground hazelnuts
¼ cup plain flour
2 tablespoons Crème de Cacao
SNOWBALL TOPPING
⅔ cup thickened cream
300g white chocolate, grated
PASSIONFRUIT SAUCE
⅔ cup passionfruit pulp
2 tablespoons castor sugar
½ cup water
2 teaspoons cornflour
1 tablespoon water, extra**

Grease 8 rounded metal moulds (½ cup capacity). Beat butter, jam and sugar in small bowl with electric mixer until light and creamy; add egg yolks, beat until combined.
  Transfer mixture to large bowl, stir in cooled chocolate, hazelnuts and sifted flour. Beat egg whites in small bowl with electric mixer until soft peaks form, lightly fold into chocolate mixture in 2 batches. Spoon cake mixture evenly into prepared moulds.

Place moulds on oven tray, bake in moderate oven for about 20 minutes or until cakes are firm; stand for 5 minutes, turn onto wire rack to cool.

When cakes are cold, sprinkle with liqueur, spread with snowball topping; serve with sauce.

Snowball Topping: Place cream in small saucepan, bring to boil, remove from heat, stir in chocolate, stir until smooth. Pour into medium bowl; cool until just beginning to thicken; beat until thick and spreadable.

Passionfruit Sauce: Combine passionfruit, sugar and water in small saucepan. Blend cornflour with extra water in small bowl, stir into passionfruit mixture, stir over high heat until mixture boils and thickens. Strain sauce, return 3 teaspoons of seeds to strained sauce, discard remaining seeds, refrigerate passionfruit sauce before serving.

Serves 8.

LEFT: Fresh Tangerine Jelly.
ABOVE: Double Chocolate Snowballs.

Above: Plate from Studio-Haus; column from John Normyle.
Left: Plate from Wedgwood; basket from Appley Hoare Antiques.

TUILES WITH BLUEBERRY LIQUEUR CREAM

Tuiles are wafer-thin biscuits. Cointreau is an orange-flavoured liqueur. Assemble desserts 3 hours before serving; keep, covered, in refrigerator. Tuiles unsuitable to freeze or microwave.

1 egg white
¼ cup castor sugar
2 tablespoons plain flour
30g butter, melted
½ teaspoon vanilla essence
BLUEBERRY SAUCE
200g punnet blueberries
2 tablespoons icing sugar
1 tablespoon Cointreau
BLUEBERRY CREAM
300ml carton thickened cream
⅓ cup icing sugar
200g punnet blueberries

Beat egg white in small bowl with electric mixer until soft peaks form, gradually add sugar, beat well between additions. Fold in sifted flour, butter and essence.

Place heaped teaspoons of mixture about 10cm apart on lightly greased oven tray. Use back of teaspoon to spread mixture to about 5cm diameter. Bake in moderate oven for about 5 minutes or until lightly browned around the edges. Lift tuiles carefully from tray onto wire racks to cool. You will need 16 tuiles for this recipe.

Pour sauce onto plates, place a tuile in centre of each plate, spread with blueberry cream, top with another tuile, repeat with remaining cream and tuiles, finishing with a tuile. Serve dusted with sifted icing sugar, if desired.

Blueberry Sauce: Blend or process all ingredients until smooth.
Blueberry Cream: Beat cream in small bowl until soft peaks form, fold in sifted icing sugar and blueberries.

Serves 4.

RIGHT: Tuiles with Blueberry Liqueur Cream.
ABOVE: Chocolate Orange Cups.

Right: Plates from Studio-Haus
Above: Plate from Studio-Haus

CHOCOLATE ORANGE CUPS

Desserts are best made 3 hours ahead; keep, covered, in refrigerator. This recipe is not suitable to freeze or microwave.

250g packet sponge finger biscuits
ORANGE SYRUP
½ cup water
¼ cup orange juice
⅓ cup castor sugar
CHOCOLATE FILLING
100g dark chocolate, chopped
60g butter, chopped
2 eggs, separated
¼ cup icing sugar

Line 4 straight-sided moulds (1 cup capacity) with foil.

Cut sponge fingers in half crossways, cut each half into 3 lengthways. Brush sponge finger lengths all over with orange syrup. Line base of each mould with 3 lengths of sponge fingers, trim to fit. Line sides of moulds with remaining sponge finger lengths, trim level with top of mould.

Spoon filling evenly into moulds, cover, refrigerate until firm. Turn onto plate, serve with whipped cream, if desired.

Orange Syrup: Combine water, juice and sugar in small saucepan, stir over heat, without boiling, until sugar is dissolved, bring to boil, boil, without stirring, uncovered for 3 minutes; cool.

Chocolate Filling: Combine chocolate and butter in medium bowl, stir over simmering water until melted; cool 5 minutes. Stir in egg yolks. Beat egg whites in small bowl with electric mixer until soft peaks form, gradually add sifted icing sugar, fold into chocolate mixture in 2 batches.

Serves 4.

BERRY MOULDS WITH FRUIT SAUCE

Recipe can be made 2 days ahead; keep, covered, in refrigerator. This recipe is not suitable to freeze.

**250g fresh or frozen raspberries
1 medium pear, chopped
1 tablespoon cherry brandy
1 tablespoon lemon juice
3 eggs, separated
¼ cup castor sugar
1½ tablespoons gelatine
⅓ cup water
300ml carton thickened cream
FRUIT SAUCE
125g fresh or frozen raspberries
½ cup apple and cherry juice
¼ cup water
2 tablespoons castor sugar
1 tablespoon cherry brandy
½ teaspoon gelatine
2 teaspoons water, extra**

Lightly oil 8 moulds (½ cup capacity). Blend or process berries, pear, brandy and juice until smooth; strain mixture into small saucepan. Bring to boil (or microwave on HIGH for 2 minutes), remove from heat, cool mixture until warm.

Combine egg yolks and sugar in top of double saucepan (or heatproof bowl), whisk over simmering water until mixture is pale and thick; transfer to large bowl. Gradually whisk in berry mixture.

Sprinkle gelatine over water in small bowl, stand in small pan of simmering water, stir until dissolved (or microwave on HIGH for about 30 seconds), cool. Stir gelatine mixture into berry mixture.

Beat cream in small bowl, fold into berry mixture. Beat egg whites in small bowl until soft peaks form, lightly fold into berry mixture in 2 batches.

Pour mixture into prepared moulds, refrigerate until set. Turn moulds onto plates, serve with sauce and extra fruit, if desired.

Fruit Sauce: Blend or process berries, juice, water, sugar and brandy until smooth; strain. Sprinkle gelatine over extra water in small bowl, stand in small pan of simmering water, stir until dissolved (or microwave on HIGH for about 10 seconds), cool. Stir gelatine mixture into berry mixture; refrigerate several hours.

Serves 8.

COFFEE LIQUEUR BLANCMANGE

Kahlua is a coffee-flavoured liqueur. Blancmange can be made a day ahead; keep, covered in refrigerator. Recipe not suitable to freeze or microwave.

**¼ cup cornflour
2 tablespoons castor sugar
2½ cups milk
¼ cup Kahlua**

Blend cornflour and sugar in medium saucepan with a little of the milk, stir in remaining milk. Stir over high heat until mixture boils and thickens. Stir in liqueur; pour into 4 glasses (¾ cup capacity), cover surface of each blancmange with plastic wrap to prevent skin forming, refrigerate until set. Serve with whipped cream and grated chocolate, if desired.

Serves 4.

ABOVE: Berry Moulds with Fruit Sauce.
RIGHT: From top: Spiced Peach Fool with Coconut Wafers, Coffee Liqueur Blancmange.

*Right: Bowls from Shop 3 Balmain;
Chest from Country Furniture Antiques*

SPICED PEACH FOOL WITH COCONUT WAFERS

Dessert can be made a day ahead; keep, covered, in refrigerator. Wafers will keep in airtight container in refrigerator for several weeks. This recipe is not suitable to freeze or microwave.

10 medium (1kg) peaches, peeled, stoned
¼ cup castor sugar
2 tablespoons honey
1 tablespoon lemon juice
1 teaspoon ground nutmeg
2 tablespoons arrowroot
2 tablespoons water
½ cup sour cream
COCONUT WAFERS
30g butter
1½ tablespoons castor sugar
1½ teaspoons honey
1 teaspoon lemon juice
1 tablespoon plain flour
2 tablespoons coconut

Blend or process peaches, sugar, honey, juice and nutmeg until smooth; pour into medium saucepan. Blend arrowroot with water, stir into peach mixture, stir over heat until mixture boils and thickens; cool.

Stir cream into peach mixture, pour into 8 glasses (½ cup capacity), refrigerate for several hours. Serve with coconut wafers, cream and fruit, if desired.

Coconut Wafers: Beat butter and sugar in small bowl with electric mixer until light and fluffy. Beat in honey and juice, fold in sifted flour and coconut. Place level teaspoons of mixture about 5cm apart on lightly greased oven trays. Bake in moderately slow oven for about 15 minutes or until wafers are golden brown. Stand wafers on tray for about 1 minute or until almost set, carefully remove to wire racks to cool.

Serves 8.

RIGHT: Blueberry Delights with Orange Liqueur Cream.
FAR RIGHT: Mandarin Compote with Champagne.

Right: Glass and plate from Shop 3, Balmain; plant from Liquidamber Nursery.
Far right: Bowl from Kosta Boda; tiles from Northbridge Ceramic & Marble Centre

BLUEBERRY DELIGHTS WITH ORANGE LIQUEUR CREAM

Cointreau is an orange-flavoured liqueur. Desserts are best made several hours ahead; keep, covered, in refrigerator. This recipe is not suitable to freeze.

**2 x 200g punnets blueberries
½ cup castor sugar
½ cup water
2 teaspoons grated orange rind
2 tablespoons orange juice
2 teaspoons gelatine
2 tablespoons water, extra
ORANGE LIQUEUR CREAM
300ml carton thickened cream
¼ cup icing sugar
2 teaspoons grated orange rind
2 teaspoons Cointreau**

Combine berries, sugar, water, rind and juice in medium saucepan, stir over heat, without boiling, until sugar is dissolved, bring to boil, reduce heat, simmer, uncovered, for 10 minutes.

Sprinkle gelatine over extra water in small bowl, stand in small pan of simmering water, stir until dissolved (or microwave on HIGH for 20 seconds). Stir gelatine mixture into berry mixture. Pour into 4 glasses (1 cup capacity), refrigerate until set. Serve with orange cream.

Orange Liqueur Cream: Beat cream and sifted icing sugar in small bowl until soft peaks form, fold in rind and liqueur; refrigerate 30 minutes.

Serves 4.

MANDARIN COMPOTE WITH CHAMPAGNE

Compôte and crème anglaise can be made a day ahead; keep, covered, in refrigerator. This recipe is not suitable to freeze or microwave.

**4 medium mandarins
1 cup water
⅓ cup strained orange juice
½ cup sugar
1 tablespoon honey
1 cinnamon stick
⅓ cup champagne
CREME ANGLAISE
4 egg yolks
⅓ cup castor sugar
2 cups milk
1 vanilla bean**

Remove membranes from mandarin segments.

Combine water, juice, sugar, honey and cinnamon in medium saucepan, stir over heat, without boiling, until sugar is dissolved. Bring to boil, boil, uncovered, without stirring, for 3 minutes, reduce heat, add mandarin segments, simmer, uncovered, for 3 minutes. Remove from heat, transfer mixture to large bowl, stir in champagne, refrigerate for several hours. Remove cinnamon. Serve compôte with crème anglaise.

Crème Anglaise: Combine egg yolks and sugar in medium bowl, beat with electric mixer until thick and creamy. Combine milk and vanilla bean in medium saucepan, bring to boil; remove from heat, stir into egg mixture, return to pan, stir over heat, without boiling, until custard thickens slightly; strain.

Serves 6.

PLUM TERRINE WITH SABAYON CREAM

Terrine can be made a day ahead; keep, covered, in refrigerator. Sabayon cream can be made several hours ahead; keep, covered, in refrigerator. Grand Marnier is an orange-flavoured liqueur. Recipe unsuitable to freeze.

1¼kg blood plums, stoned, chopped
1¼ cups castor sugar
2 teaspoons grated orange rind
1 cup orange juice
¼ cup Grand Marnier
3 tablespoons gelatine
½ cup water
½ cup pine nuts
SABAYON CREAM
1½ tablespoons castor sugar
1 tablespoon water
2 eggs yolks
2 teaspoons Grand Marnier
½ cup thickened cream

Line deep rectangular dish (6 cup capacity) with plastic wrap.

Combine plums, sugar, rind, juice and liqueur in large saucepan, stir over heat, without boiling, until sugar is dissolved. Bring to boil, reduce heat, cover, simmer for about 15 minutes (or microwave on HIGH for about 15 minutes) or until plums are soft.

Sprinkle gelatine over water in small bowl, stand in small pan of simmering water, stir until dissolved (or microwave on HIGH for about 1 minute). Stir gelatine mixture into plum mixture; refrigerate until beginning to set; stir in nuts.

Pour plum mixture into prepared dish, cover, refrigerate for several hours or until set. Turn terrine onto plate, remove plastic wrap, serve sliced with sabayon cream.

Sabayon Cream: Combine sugar and water in small saucepan, stir over heat, without boiling, until sugar is dissolved, bring to boil, remove from heat. Beat yolks in top of double saucepan (or in heatproof bowl) with electric mixer over simmering water until thick and creamy, gradually beat in hot sugar syrup, remove from heat, cool to room temperature. Stir in liqueur. Beat cream in small bowl until firm peaks form, fold into egg mixture.

Serves 8.

BANANAS WITH PEANUT CARAMEL CREAM

Caramel can be made a day ahead; keep, covered, in refrigerator. Recipe unsuitable to freeze or microwave.

125g butter
1 cup brown sugar, firmly packed
400g can sweetened condensed milk
¼ cup sour cream
⅓ cup thickened cream
¼ cup smooth peanut butter
6 medium bananas
2 tablespoons lime juice

Melt butter in medium saucepan, stir in sugar and milk, stir over heat, without boiling, until sugar is dissolved. Stir over high heat for about 5 minutes or until mixture is golden brown. Remove from heat, allow bubbles to subside.

Gradually stir in creams and peanut butter; cool. Refrigerate before using. Slice bananas, combine with juice in medium bowl. Divide mixture between 6 glasses (1 cup capacity). Spoon peanut caramel cream over bananas, serve with extra whipped cream, if desired.

Serves 6.

LEFT: Plum Terrine with Sabayon Cream.
RIGHT: Bananas with Peanut Caramel Cream.

Left: Plate and fork from Studio-Haus. Right: Glasses from Shop 3, Balmain; background screen from Mr Brassman

SUMMER FRUIT PUDDING

Framboise is a raspberry-flavoured liqueur. For best results use a traditional unsliced sandwich loaf. Pudding is best made a day ahead; keep, covered, in refrigerator. This recipe is not suitable to freeze.

10 thick slices white bread
250g punnet strawberries
250g punnet raspberries
250g punnet red currants
¾ cup castor sugar
1 tablespoon Framboise

Line pudding mould (4 cup capacity) with foil.

Trim crusts from bread, reserve 2 slices, cut remaining slices into 3 fingers. Line base of mould with 1 reserved slice, cut to fit base. Line sides of mould with some of the bread fingers, overlapping slightly.

Combine berries, currants and sugar in medium saucepan, stir over heat, without boiling, until sugar is dissolved. Bring to boil, reduce heat, cover, simmer for about 3 minutes, or until fruit softens. Stir in liqueur, strain, reserve liquid and fruit.

Brush bread in mould with some of the reserved liquid. Spoon fruit into mould, top with reserved bread slice and fingers. Pour remaining liquid over bread. Cover pudding with foil, cover with plate slightly smaller than the mould, place heavy weight on top, refrigerate overnight.

Turn pudding onto plate, serve with whipped cream, if desired.

CUSTARD APPLE AND PASSIONFRUIT FLAN

Flan can be made a day ahead; keep, covered, in refrigerator. This recipe is not suitable to freeze.

1 cup plain sweet biscuit crumbs
90g butter, melted
FILLING
1 medium (500g) custard apple
½ teaspoon grated lemon rind
1 tablespoon lemon juice
1 medium passionfruit
1 tablespoon gelatine
¼ cup water
3 eggs
½ cup castor sugar
½ cup thickened cream

Combine crumbs and butter in small bowl; mix well. Press mixture evenly over base and side of 23cm flan tin or pie plate, refrigerate while preparing filling. Pour filling into crumb crust, refrigerate for several hours or until set. Decorate with extra whipped cream and passionfruit, if desired.

Filling: Remove skin and seeds from custard apple. Blend or process custard apple with rind and juice until smooth. Transfer to medium bowl, stir in passionfruit pulp.

Sprinkle gelatine over water in small bowl, stand in small pan of simmering water, stir until dissolved (or microwave on HIGH for about 30 seconds); cool slightly; do not allow to set. Stir gelatine into fruit mixture.

Beat eggs in small bowl with electric mixer until thick and creamy, gradually add sugar, beat until dissolved. Beat cream in small bowl until soft peaks form. Fold egg mixture and cream into fruit mixture.

BELOW LEFT: Summer Fruit Pudding.
BELOW: Custard Apple and Passionfruit Flan.

CHOCOLATE BAGS WITH CHERRY LIQUEUR CREAM

Cherry Advocaat is a cherry-flavoured liqueur. We used 6 x 8cm x 10cm paper lolly bags for this recipe. Chocolate bags can be made a week ahead; keep, covered, in refrigerator. Fill with cream just before serving. This recipe is not suitable to freeze.

**200g dark chocolate, melted
300ml carton thickened cream
2 tablespoons icing sugar
2½ tablespoons Cherry Advocaat**

Brush inside of each bag with a thick layer of chocolate, freeze until set. Brush with another layer of chocolate, freeze until set. Peel paper bag away from chocolate, refrigerate.
 Combine cream, sifted icing sugar and liqueur in small bowl, beat with electric mixer until soft peaks form. Place chocolate bags onto plates, pipe or spoon cream into each bag, refrigerate for 1 hour before serving.
 Makes 6.

CUMQUAT SYLLABUB

Syllabub is best made just before serving. You will need about 100g cumquats for this recipe. This recipe is not suitable to freeze or microwave.

**1 tablespoon cumquat juice
1 teaspoon chopped cumquat rind
1 tablespoon brandy
½ cup castor sugar
300ml carton thickened cream**

Combine juice, rind, brandy and sugar in small saucepan, stir over heat, without boiling, until sugar is dissolved; cool, strain.
 Beat cream and cumquat syrup in small bowl with electric mixer until soft peaks form. Spoon mixture into 4 glasses (½ cup capacity), serve with sponge fingers and brandied cumquats, if desired.
 Serves 4.

LEFT: Chocolate Bags with Cherry Liqueur Cream.
BELOW: Cumquat Syllabub.

Below: Plate from Villeroy & Boch; glass from Village Living

MANDARINS JUBILEE

You will need about 3 large mandarins, extra, for the juice. Grand Marnier is an orange-flavoured liqueur. Dessert is best made just before serving. This recipe is not suitable to freeze.

**3 medium mandarins
1 cup mandarin juice
2 tablespoons castor sugar
2 teaspoons arrowroot
¼ cup water
2 tablespoons Grand Marnier**

Segment mandarins by removing all membranes.
   Combine juice and sugar in medium saucepan, bring to boil, reduce heat, simmer, uncovered, for 2 minutes (or microwave on HIGH for 3 minutes).
   Blend arrowroot with water in small bowl, stir into juice mixture, stir over high heat (or microwave on HIGH for about 3 minutes) until mixture boils and thickens, stir in mandarin segments. Warm liqueur in small saucepan, pour over hot mandarin mixture, set aflame. Serve with ice cream, if desired.
   Serves 4.

CUSTARD APPLE FRUIT SALAD

Fruit salad is best made on day of serving; keep, covered, in refrigerator. This recipe is not suitable to freeze.

**2 large custard apples
1 small rockmelon
250g punnet strawberries, halved
HONEY AND LEMON SYRUP
2 tablespoons honey
2 tablespoons lemon juice**

Cut custard apples into large pieces. Scoop small balls from rockmelon. Combine custard apples, rockmelon and strawberries in large bowl, pour syrup over fruit. Cover, refrigerate for 1 hour before serving.
Honey and Lemon Syrup: Combine ingredients in a small bowl.
   Serves 4.

COCONUT SNAP HORNS WITH CARDAMOM CREAM

Horns can be made a day ahead; keep in airtight container. Fill horns just before serving. This recipe is not suitable to freeze or microwave.

**¼ cup golden syrup
90g butter
⅓ cup brown sugar
¼ cup plain flour
1 teaspoon ground ginger
1 teaspoon ground cinnamon
¼ cup coconut
100g dark chocolate, melted**

CARDAMOM CREAM
2 x 300ml cartons thickened cream
¾ teaspoon ground cardamom
¾ teaspoon ground ginger
1 tablespoon icing sugar
⅓ cup chopped glacé ginger

Combine golden syrup, butter and sugar in medium saucepan, stir over heat until butter is melted. Remove from heat, stir in combined sifted flour, ginger, cinnamon and coconut. Drop 2 heaped teaspoons of mixture about 8cm apart on lightly greased oven tray. For easy handling, bake 2 at a time. Bake in moderate oven for about 6 minutes or until golden brown. Stand snaps on tray for about 1 minute or until starting to set, lift carefully from tray with spatula. Wrap each snap around 14cm long cream horn mould; cool, remove from moulds. Dip open edges of horns in chocolate. When set, fill with cardamom cream.

Cardamom Cream: Whip cream, cardamom, ground ginger and sifted icing sugar in small bowl with electric mixer until soft peaks form, fold in glacé ginger.

Makes 12.

TOP LEFT: Mandarins Jubilee.
LEFT: Custard Apple Fruit Salad.
ABOVE: Coconut Snap Horns with Cardamom Cream.

Left: Bowl from Kosta Boda

CHOCOLATE CHESTNUT CASES WITH STRAWBERRY SAUCE

Make cases by placing 3 paper patty cases inside each other to give the strength required to hold the chocolate. Cases and sauce can be made a day ahead; keep, covered, in refrigerator. Prepare chestnut cream just before serving. This recipe is not suitable to freeze or microwave.

200g dark chocolate, melted
CHESTNUT CREAM
300ml carton thickened cream
250g can chestnut spread
2 tablespoons underproof dark rum
1 egg white
STRAWBERRY SAUCE
250g punnet strawberries
2 teaspoons cornflour
¾ cup water
2 tablespoons castor sugar

Spread chocolate evenly over base and side of each set of patty cases, place cases upside-down on lightly oiled tray, refrigerate until set. Carefully peel paper away from chocolate cases.

Spoon chestnut cream into piping bag fitted with fluted tube, pipe into chocolate cases. Serve topped with reserved strawberries and sauce.

Chestnut Cream: Beat cream, chestnut spread, rum and egg white in

CREAM HEARTS WITH BERRY SAUCE

We used coeur a la crème moulds in this recipe; these have draining holes in the base. Any berries can be used in this recipe. Dessert can be made 2 days ahead; keep, covered, in refrigerator. This recipe is not suitable to freeze.

250g ricotta cheese
2 tablespoons castor sugar
1 teaspoon almond essence
2 teaspoons grated lime rind
⅔ cup sour cream
½ cup thickened cream, whipped
BERRY SAUCE
250g fresh or frozen boysenberries
2 tablespoons castor sugar
¾ cup water
1 teaspoon cornflour
2 teaspoons water, extra

Beat cheese, sugar, essence and rind in small bowl with electric mixer until smooth; stir in sour cream, then fold in cream. Line 4 moulds (⅔ cup capacity) with muslin. Spoon cheese mixture into lined moulds, fold over excess muslin to cover top of cheese mixture, place moulds on tray, refrigerate overnight. Unmould desserts onto plates, serve with berry sauce.

Berry Sauce: Combine berries, sugar and water in medium saucepan, bring to boil, reduce heat, simmer for about 5 minutes or until berries are just soft. Blend cornflour with extra water, stir into berry mixture, stir over high heat until mixture boils and thickens. Press mixture through sieve; cool.

Serves 4.

LEFT: Chocolate Chestnut Cases with Strawberry Sauce.
BELOW: Cream Hearts with Berry Sauce.

Left: Tiles from Northbridge Ceramic & Marble Centre

small bowl with electric mixer until firm peaks form.

Strawberry Sauce: Halve 10 strawberries; reserve remaining strawberries. Blend or process remaining strawberries until smooth. Blend cornflour with 1 tablespoon of the water in small saucepan, stir in strawberry purée, remaining water and sugar. Stir over high heat until sauce boils and thickens. Cool; refrigerate.

Makes 10.

MANGO CREAMS

Cointreau is an orange-flavoured liqueur. Creams can be made 2 days ahead; keep, covered, in refrigerator. You will need about 5 medium mangoes for this recipe. Recipe unsuitable to freeze.

**2 cups chopped fresh mango
2 tablespoons Cointreau
½ cup orange juice
1 tablespoon gelatine
½ cup water
½ cup thickened cream
2 egg whites
1 tablespoon castor sugar**

Lightly oil 8 moulds (⅓ cup capacity). Blend or process mango, liqueur and juice until smooth, transfer to large bowl. Sprinkle gelatine over water in small bowl, stand in small pan of simmering water, stir until dissolved (or microwave on HIGH for about 40 seconds); cool. Stir gelatine mixture into mango mixture.

Beat cream in small bowl until soft peaks form, fold cream into mango mixture. Beat egg whites in small bowl with electric mixer until soft peaks form, add sugar, beat until sugar is dissolved. Fold egg white mixture into mango mixture. Pour into prepared moulds, refrigerate until set. Turn onto plates, serve with extra cream and toasted almonds, if desired.

Serves 8.

CUSTARD APPLE COCONUT YOGURT

Dessert is best made just before serving. Recipe unsuitable to freeze.

**1 medium (500g) custard apple
½ cup plain yogurt
⅓ cup coconut milk
1 tablespoon honey**

Blend or process custard apple until smooth; push through sieve. Combine custard apple purée, yogurt, milk and honey in medium bowl; mix well. Serve with fresh fruit of your choice.

Serves 6.

FRUIT SALAD RING

Grand Marnier is an orange-flavoured liqueur. Dessert can be made a day ahead; keep, covered, in refrigerator. This recipe is not suitable to freeze.

**4 tablespoons gelatine
1 litre (4 cups) clear apple juice
½ cup sweet white wine
¼ cup Grand Marnier
250g punnet strawberries, halved
200g punnet blueberries
2 medium oranges, segmented
1 medium kiwi fruit, chopped**

Sprinkle gelatine over 1 cup of the juice in medium bowl, stand in medium pan of simmering water, stir until dissolved (or microwave on HIGH for about 1 minute). Cool to room temperature; do not allow to set.

Combine the gelatine mixture, remaining juice, wine and liqueur in large bowl. Combine berries, oranges and kiwi fruit in large bowl. Pour ¼ cup juice mixture into ring mould (7 cup capacity), spoon in one-quarter of fruit mixture; refrigerate until set. Repeat layers until all the mixture and fruit have been used. Refrigerate for several hours or until set.

Serves 8.

LEFT: From top: Custard Apple Coconut Yogurt, Mango Creams.
BELOW: Fruit Salad Ring.

*Left: Fruit bowl and glass bowls from Village Living.
Below: Plate from Villeroy & Boch; tiles from Northbridge Ceramic & Marble Centre*

TOFFEE LATTICE WITH FRESH FRUIT

You will need about 4 passionfruit for this recipe. Dessert should be prepared close to serving time. This recipe is not suitable to freeze or microwave.

**¾ cup castor sugar
2 tablespoons water
fresh fruit
PASSIONFRUIT CREME ANGLAISE
2 tablespoons castor sugar
2 egg yolks
½ cup milk
½ cup cream
1 teaspoon cornflour
1 teaspoon custard powder
¼ cup milk, extra
2 tablespoons passionfruit pulp**

Lightly oil outside of 6 rounded metal moulds (1 cup capacity).

Combine sugar and water in medium heavy-based saucepan, stir over heat, without boiling, until sugar is dissolved. Bring to boil, boil, uncovered, without stirring, for about 10 minutes or until toffee is golden brown and a teaspoon of toffee mixture cracks when dropped into a cup of cold water. Stand toffee away from heat for about 2 minutes or until slightly thickened.

Drizzle toffee over outside of moulds; allow to set. Carefully remove lattice from moulds. Pour crème anglaise onto plates, add fruit of your choice, top with toffee lattice.

Passionfruit Crème Anglaise: Beat sugar and egg yolks in small bowl with electric mixer until thick and creamy. Combine milk and cream in small saucepan, bring to boil, beat hot milk mixture into egg yolk mixture while motor is operating; return to pan.

Blend cornflour and custard powder with extra milk in small bowl, stir into hot milk mixture. Stir over high heat until mixture boils and thickens, stir in passionfruit, cover, cool to room temperature; refrigerate.

Serves 6.

RIGHT: Toffee Lattice with Fresh Fruit.

Right: Fork from Made Where

STRAWBERRY MOUSSE WITH TROPICAL SAUCE

Cointreau is an orange-flavoured liqueur. You will need about 6 passionfruit for this recipe. Mousse and sauce can be made a day ahead; keep, covered, in refrigerator. This recipe is not suitable to freeze.

2 x 250g punnets strawberries
⅓ cup castor sugar
2 tablespoons Cointreau
2 tablespoons gelatine
⅓ cup water
300ml carton thickened cream
TROPICAL SAUCE
⅓ cup castor sugar
½ cup water
2 teaspoons grated orange rind
½ cup orange juice
½ cup fresh passionfruit pulp

Lightly oil 14cm x 21cm loaf dish. Blend or process strawberries, sugar and liqueur until smooth; transfer mixture to large bowl.

Sprinkle gelatine over water in small bowl, stand in small pan of simmering water stir until dissolved (or microwave on HIGH for about 30 seconds); cool to room temperature.

Stir gelatine into strawberry mixture. Beat cream in small bowl until soft peaks form, fold lightly into strawberry mixture. Pour mousse into prepared dish, cover, refrigerate until set. Serve with sauce.

Tropical Sauce: Combine sugar, water, rind and juice in small saucepan, stir over heat, without boiling, until sugar is dissolved. Bring to boil, boil, uncovered, without stirring, for about 10 minutes or until reduced by half. Stir in passionfruit; cool.

LIME AND JELLY BAVARIAN

Bavarian can be made a day ahead; keep, covered, in refrigerator. This recipe is not suitable to freeze.

3 egg yolks
½ cup castor sugar
⅔ cup milk
1 teaspoon grated lime rind
⅓ cup lime juice
2 teaspoons gelatine
300ml carton thickened cream
green food colouring
LIME JELLY
1 teaspoon gelatine
¼ cup lime juice
⅓ cup water
¼ cup castor sugar

Beat egg yolks and sugar in small bowl with electric mixer until thick and creamy. Heat milk in small saucepan until almost boiling, gradually beat into egg mixture while motor is operating. Return mixture to pan, stir over heat, without boiling, until mixture thickens slightly, strain; stir in rind and ¼ cup of the juice.

Sprinkle gelatine over remaining juice in small bowl, stand in small pan of simmering water, stir until dissolved (or microwave on HIGH for about 15 seconds). Stir gelatine mixture into lime juice mixture; transfer to medium bowl. Refrigerate until mixture is the consistency of unbeaten egg white.

Beat cream in small bowl until firm peaks form, fold into lime mixture, tint with colouring. Pour mixture into 4 glasses (1 cup capacity), refrigerate until set. Top with lime jelly, refrigerate until set. Decorate with extra cream and shredded lime rind, if desired.

Lime Jelly: Sprinkle gelatine over juice in small bowl, stand in small pan of simmering water, stir until dissolved (or microwave on HIGH for about 30 seconds). Combine water and sugar in small saucepan, stir over heat, without boiling, until sugar is dissolved, stir in gelatine mixture, tint with colouring, if desired, cool to room temperature before using.

Serves 4.

GLACE GINGER AND PEACH MOUSSE

Mousse and sauce can be made a day ahead; keep, covered, in refrigerator. This recipe is not suitable to freeze.

3 eggs, separated
¼ cup castor sugar
1½ cups milk
1 tablespoon gelatine
¼ cup water
300ml carton thickened cream
¼ cup chopped glacé ginger
¼ cup chopped glacé peaches
GINGER SAUCE
1 cup water
½ cup golden syrup
¼ cup chopped glacé ginger
2 teaspoons cornflour
2 teaspoons water, extra

Lightly oil ring mould (5 cup capacity).

Beat egg yolks and sugar in small bowl with electric mixer until thick and creamy. Heat milk in medium saucepan until lukewarm; beat into egg mixture while motor is operating, return mixture to pan. Stir over heat, without boiling, until mixture is slightly thickened. Transfer to large bowl.

Sprinkle gelatine over water in small bowl, stand in small pan of simmering water, stir until dissolved (or microwave on HIGH for about 30 seconds). Stir gelatine mixture into egg mixture, cool to room temperature; do not allow to set.

Beat cream in small bowl until soft peaks form; stir in ginger and peaches. Fold cream mixture into egg mixture.

Beat egg whites in small bowl with electric mixer until firm peaks form, fold into egg mixture, pour into prepared mould. Refrigerate until set. Turn onto plate, sprinkle with extra peaches, if desired, serve with sauce.

Ginger Sauce: Blend or process water, golden syrup and ginger until smooth, pour into small saucepan. Blend cornflour with extra water; stir into ginger mixture, stir over high heat until mixture boils and thickens slightly. Cool before serving.

RIGHT: Back, from left: Lime and Jelly Bavarian, Strawberry Mousse with Tropical Sauce. Front: Glacé Ginger and Peach Mousse.

CARAMEL SOUFFLES WITH WALNUT PRALINE

Soufflés can be made a day ahead; keep, covered, in refrigerator. Decorate sides of soufflés with praline just before serving. This recipe is not suitable to freeze.

3 eggs, separated
½ cup brown sugar
1 tablespoon gelatine
¼ cup water
⅓ cup golden syrup
300ml carton thickened cream
WALNUT PRALINE
¼ cup sugar
¼ cup walnut pieces

Place a collar of foil around 4 dishes (½ cup capacity), secure with string. Brush inside of foil lightly with oil.

Beat egg yolks and sugar in top of double saucepan (or heatproof bowl) over simmering water until thick and creamy. Sprinkle gelatine over water in small bowl, stand in small pan of simmering water, stir until dissolved (or microwave on HIGH for about 30 seconds). Stir gelatine mixture into egg mixture with golden syrup, stir over simmering water until combined. Remove mixture from heat, transfer to large bowl, cover, cool to room temperature.

Beat cream until soft peaks form, fold into caramel mixture. Beat egg whites until firm peaks form, gently fold into caramel mixture. Pour mixture into prepared dishes, refrigerate until set.

Remove collars, roll sides of soufflés in walnut praline. Decorate with whipped cream, and sprinkle with praline, if desired.

Walnut Praline: Melt sugar in small heavy-based saucepan over medium heat; do not stir. When sugar starts to brown, stir gently to dissolve remaining sugar. Spread nuts onto lightly greased oven tray, pour hot toffee evenly over nuts. When set, break into pieces, blend or process pieces until finely ground.

Serves 4.

LEFT: Caramel Soufflés with Walnut Praline.

PINA COLADA MOUSSE

Mousse can be made a day ahead; keep, covered, in refrigerator. This recipe is not suitable to freeze.

3 teaspoons gelatine
¼ cup water
1 cup drained crushed pineapple
3 eggs, separated
½ cup castor sugar
⅓ cup coconut cream
⅓ cup pineapple juice
2 tablespoons white rum
⅔ cup thickened cream

Sprinkle gelatine over water in small bowl, stand in small pan of simmering water, stir until dissolved (or microwave on HIGH for about 30 seconds). Cool to room temperature; do not allow to set.

Spoon pineapple into 4 glasses (1 cup capacity). Beat egg yolks and sugar in small bowl with electric mixer until thick and creamy. Stir in coconut cream, juice, rum and gelatine mixture. Transfer to large bowl.

Beat cream in small bowl until soft peaks form, fold into coconut cream mixture. Beat egg whites in small bowl with electric mixer until soft peaks form, fold into coconut cream mixture. Pour into glasses. Refrigerate until set. Decorate with whipped cream and toasted shredded coconut, if desired.

Serves 4.

LEFT: Pina Colada Mousse.
ABOVE: Creamy Marsala Soufflés.

Above: Plate and bowl from Villeroy & Boch; tiles from Northbridge Ceramic & Marble Centre. Left: Glasses from Dansab.

CREAMY MARSALA SOUFFLES

Soufflés can be made a day ahead; keep, covered, in refrigerator. This recipe is not suitable to freeze.

3 egg yolks
⅓ cup castor sugar
¾ cup milk
2 tablespoons marsala
3 teaspoons gelatine
¼ cup water
300ml carton thickened cream

Place a collar of foil around 4 dishes (½ cup capacity), secure with string. Brush inside of foil lightly with oil.

Beat egg yolks and sugar in small bowl with electric mixer until thick and creamy. Heat milk in small saucepan until almost boiling, gradually beat into egg yolk mixture. Return mixture to pan, stir over heat, without boiling, until mixture begins to thicken. Transfer to large bowl, stir in marsala, cover, cool to room temperature.

Sprinkle gelatine over water in small bowl, stand in small pan of simmering water, stir until dissolved (or microwave on HIGH for about 30 seconds). Cool to room temperature; do not allow to set. Stir gelatine mixture into marsala mixture.

Beat cream in small bowl until soft peaks form, fold into marsala mixture in 2 batches. Pour mixture into prepared dishes, refrigerate for several hours or overnight. Remove collars, sprinkle with sifted cocoa, if desired.

Serves 4.

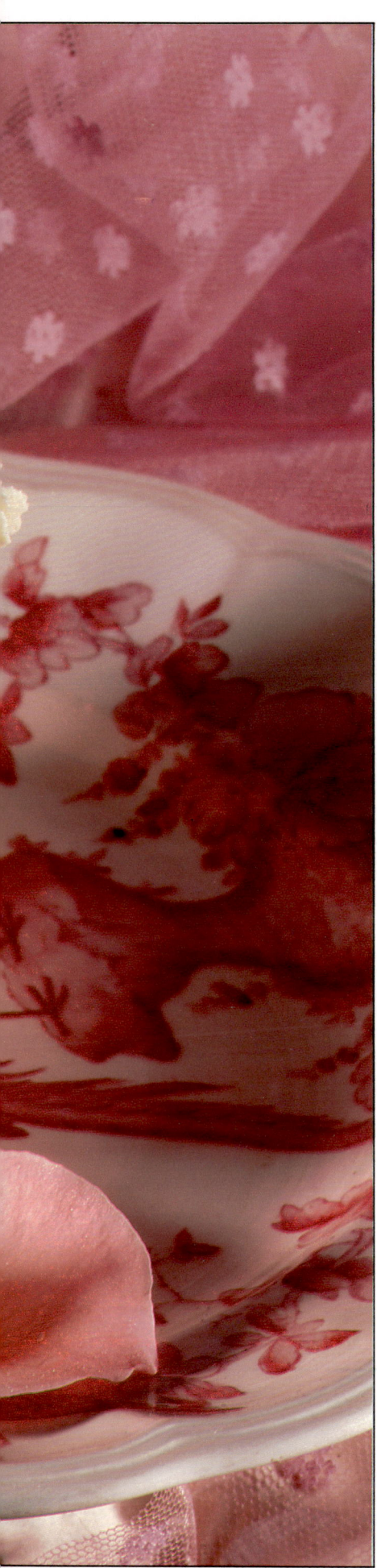

ROSEWATER SOUFFLES

Soufflés can be made a day ahead; keep, covered, in refrigerator. This recipe is not suitable to freeze.

⅓ cup castor sugar
2 tablespoons water
2 tablespoons rosewater
300ml carton thickened cream
4 egg whites
2 teaspoons gelatine
1 tablespoon water, extra
pink food colouring

Place a collar of foil around 4 dishes (½ cup capacity), secure with string.
 Combine sugar and water in small saucepan, stir over heat, without boiling, until sugar is dissolved, remove from heat, stir in rosewater; cool, refrigerate 30 minutes.
 Beat cream and sugar syrup in medium bowl until soft peaks form.
 Beat egg whites in small bowl with electric mixer until firm peaks form, fold into cream mixture. Sprinkle gelatine over extra water in small bowl, stand in small pan of simmering water, stir until dissolved (or microwave on HIGH for about 15 seconds). Fold gelatine mixture into cream mixture, tint with colouring, if desired.
 Spoon mixture into prepared dishes, refrigerate until set. Remove collars, decorate soufflés with whipped cream and rose petals, if desired.
 Serves 4.

MANGO SOUFFLES WITH CHOCOLATE COLLARS

You will need about 3 medium mangoes for this recipe. Soufflés can be made a day ahead; keep, covered, in refrigerator. This recipe is not suitable to freeze.

100g dark chocolate, melted
50g butter, melted
3 eggs, separated
⅓ cup castor sugar
½ cup milk
1½ cups fresh mango purée
1 tablespoon gelatine
¼ cup water
300ml carton thickened cream

Place a collar of foil around 6 dishes (½ cup capacity), secure with string. Brush inside of foil and half way into dishes evenly with combined chocolate and butter, refrigerate until set.
 Beat egg yolks and sugar in small bowl with electric mixer until thick and creamy. Heat milk in small saucepan until almost boiling, gradually beat into egg yolk mixture. Return mixture to pan, stir over heat, without boiling, until mixture begins to thicken. Transfer to large bowl, cover, cool to room temperature.
 Fold mango purée into custard. Sprinkle gelatine over water in small bowl, stand in small pan of simmering water (or microwave on HIGH for about 30 seconds). Cool to room temperature; do not allow to set. Stir gelatine mixture into mango mixture. Beat cream until soft peaks form, fold into mango mixture in 2 batches. Beat egg whites in small bowl until firm peaks form, fold into mango mixture. Pour into prepared dishes, refrigerate until set. Remove collars, serve decorated with whipped cream and chocolate curls, if desired.
 Serves 6.

LEFT: Rosewater Soufflés.

Left: Plate from The Country Trader.

SPICY PUMPKIN AND HAZELNUT MOUSSE

You will need to cook about 350g pumpkin for this recipe. Mousse can be made a day ahead; keep, covered, in refrigerator. This recipe is not suitable to freeze.

2½ teaspoons gelatine
⅓ cup water
½ cup castor sugar
2 teaspoons grated lemon rind
¼ cup finely chopped roasted hazelnuts
½ teaspoon ground nutmeg
½ teaspoon ground ginger
1 cup cooked mashed pumpkin
⅓ cup lemon juice
4 egg whites

Sprinkle gelatine over water in small bowl, stand in small pan of simmering water, stir until dissolved (or microwave on HIGH for about 30 seconds); cool. Blend or process sugar, rind, nuts, spices, pumpkin, juice and gelatine mixture until smooth, transfer mixture to large bowl.

Beat egg whites in small bowl with electric mixer until soft peaks form, fold into pumpkin mixture. Pour mousse into 6 dishes (¾ cup capacity). Refrigerate until firm. Serve topped with whipped cream and ground hazelnuts, if desired.

Serves 6.

RIGHT: Spicy Pumpkin and Hazelnut Mousse.
BELOW: Mango Soufflés with Chocolate Collars.

Right: Spoon from The Bay Tree; cane chair from The Australian East India Co.

LEFT: Lime and Mint Sorbet.
BELOW: Lime and Pear Ice Cream with Poached Pears.

Left: Plate from Dansab; table from Empire Studios

LIME AND MINT SORBET

You will need about 6 medium limes for this recipe. Sorbet can be made 3 days ahead; keep, covered, in freezer. This recipe is not suitable to microwave.

½ cup sugar
1¼ cups water
1 teaspoon grated lime rind
1 cup fresh lime juice
2 tablespoons chopped fresh mint
2 egg whites

Combine sugar and water in small saucepan, stir over heat, without boiling, until sugar is dissolved. Bring to boil, reduce heat, simmer, uncovered, for 10 minutes, without stirring; cool. Stir in rind, juice and mint, pour into lamington pan; cover, freeze until firm.

Remove sorbet from pan, place in large bowl with egg whites, beat with electric mixer (or beat in processor) until smooth. Return mixture to pan, cover, freeze overnight.

Serves 4.

LIME AND PEAR ICE CREAM WITH POACHED PEARS

You will need about 4 medium limes for this recipe. Ice cream can be made 3 days ahead; keep, covered, in freezer.

5 egg yolks
½ cup castor sugar
1 cup milk
2 medium pears, peeled, chopped
⅓ cup fresh lime juice
300ml carton thickened cream
POACHED PEARS
2 medium pears
¼ cup water
¼ cup fresh lime juice
1 tablespoon sugar

Cover base and sides of 14cm x 21cm loaf pan with foil.

Beat egg yolks and sugar in small bowl with electric mixer until thick and creamy. Bring milk to boil in medium saucepan, remove from heat, gradually stir in egg yolk mixture, stir over heat, without boiling, until mixture thickens slightly. Transfer mixture to large bowl, beat with electric mixer for about 15 minutes or until mixture thickens.

Blend or process pears and juice until smooth, fold into custard mixture. Beat cream in small bowl until soft peaks form, fold into pear mixture. Pour mixture into prepared pan, cover, freeze overnight. Serve ice cream with poached pears.

Poached Pears: Peel, quarter, core and slice pears. Combine water, juice and sugar in medium saucepan, bring to boil, add pears, reduce heat, cover, simmer for about 5 minutes (or microwave on HIGH for about 5 minutes) or until pears are just tender; drain. Serve warm or cold.

Serves 6.

APRICOT ICE CREAM WITH CHOC COCONUT SAUCE

Ice cream can be made 2 weeks ahead; keep, covered, in freezer. Sauce can be made a day ahead; keep, covered, in refrigerator. This recipe is not suitable to microwave.

¾ cup dried apricots
½ cup water
2 tablespoons castor sugar
¼ cup castor sugar, extra
⅓ cup water, extra
3 egg yolks
300ml carton thickened cream
CHOC COCONUT SAUCE
60g dark Choc Melts
½ cup cream
¼ cup coconut

Combine apricots and water in small saucepan, bring to boil, reduce heat, simmer, covered, for about 10 minutes or until apricots are soft. Blend or process apricot mixture until smooth, add sugar, process until combined; cool to room temperature.

Combine extra sugar and extra water in small saucepan, stir over heat, without boiling, until sugar is dissolved. Bring to boil, boil, uncovered, for 3 minutes, without stirring. Beat egg yolks in small bowl, gradually beat in hot syrup; beat until thick and creamy; transfer to large bowl, fold in apricot mixture. Beat cream in small bowl until soft peaks form, fold into apricot mixture.

Pour mixture into deep 23cm cake pan, cover, freeze until edges are beginning to set. Remove ice cream from pan, beat in large bowl with electric mixer until smooth and creamy. Return mixture to pan, cover, freeze overnight. Serve with warm choc coconut sauce.

Choc Coconut Sauce: Combine all ingredients in small saucepan, stir over heat, without boiling, until pourable.

Serves 4.

LIME ICE CREAM

You will need about 3 medium limes for this recipe. Ice cream can be made 2 days ahead; keep, covered, in freezer. This recipe is not suitable to microwave.

1 teaspoon grated lime rind
⅓ cup fresh lime juice
3 eggs, lightly beaten
¼ cup castor sugar
300ml carton thickened cream
green food colouring

Combine rind and juice in small saucepan, bring to boil, boil, uncovered, without stirring, until liquid is reduced by half; cool.

Beat eggs and sugar in top of double saucepan (or medium heatproof bowl) until thick and creamy, beat over simmering water until mixture thickens slightly, remove from heat, cover; cool.

Stir lime mixture into egg mixture. Beat cream in small bowl until soft peaks form, fold into egg mixture, tint with colouring, if desired. Pour mixture into loaf pan, cover, freeze overnight.

Serves 4.

ABOVE: From left: Apricot Ice Cream with Choc Coconut Sauce, Lime Ice Cream.

Above: Glass dishes from Dansab; stand from Empire Studios

ORANGE AND MANGO ICE

Ice can be made 3 days ahead; keep, covered, in freezer. This recipe is not suitable to microwave.

- **½ cup sugar**
- **½ cup water**
- **¼ cup dry white wine**
- **2 medium mangoes, chopped**
- **2 cups orange juice**
- **2 egg whites**

Combine sugar, water and wine in medium saucepan, stir over heat, without boiling, until sugar is dissolved, bring to boil, reduce heat, simmer, uncovered, for 10 minutes, without stirring; cool.

Blend or process mangoes and juice until smooth, stir into sugar syrup. Pour mixture into large loaf pan, cover, freeze until firm.

Remove ice from pan, beat in large bowl with electric mixer until smooth. Beat egg whites in small bowl with electric mixer until firm peaks form, fold into mango mixture. Return mixture to pan, cover, freeze until firm.

Serves 4.

PUMPKIN AND MAPLE ICE CREAM

You will need to cook about 300g pumpkin for this dessert. We used pure maple syrup in this recipe. Ice cream can be made 3 days ahead; keep, covered, in freezer.

- **6 egg yolks**
- **⅓ cup castor sugar**
- **⅓ cup maple syrup**
- **¾ cup cooked mashed pumpkin**
- **300ml carton thickened cream**
- **½ teaspoon ground nutmeg**

Beat egg yolks and sugar in small bowl with electric mixer for about 5 minutes or until thick and creamy. Gradually beat in maple syrup on low speed, then beat in pumpkin. Transfer mixture to large bowl.

Beat cream and nutmeg in small bowl until soft peaks form, fold into pumpkin mixture. Pour mixture into lamington pan, cover, freeze overnight.

Remove ice cream from freezer, chop roughly, beat in medium bowl with electric mixer until smooth. Return mixture to pan, cover, freeze until firm.

Serves 4.

BELOW: From top: Orange and Mango Ice, Pumpkin and Maple Ice Cream.

BELOW: Plates and table from The Country Trader.

CARDAMOM ICE CREAM WITH MACADAMIA TUILES

Ice cream can be made 3 days ahead; keep, covered, in freezer. Tuiles can be made 2 days ahead; keep airtight. Recipe unsuitable to microwave.

2 x 300ml cartons thickened cream
1 tablespoon cardamom pods, crushed
6 egg yolks
¾ cup castor sugar
1 teaspoon vanilla essence
MACADAMIA TUILES
1 egg white
¼ cup castor sugar
2 tablespoons plain flour
30g butter, melted
1 teaspoon vanilla essence
¼ cup roasted unsalted macadamias, finely chopped

Combine cream and cardamom in medium saucepan, bring to boil, remove from heat, cover, stand for 10 minutes, strain; discard cardamom.

Beat egg yolks and sugar in top half of double saucepan (or medium heatproof bowl), beat over simmering water until sugar is dissolved. Beat cream into egg mixture, stir over simmering water for about 10 minutes or until mixture is thickened, stir in essence; cool.

Pour mixture into deep 20cm square cake pan, cover; freeze until set. Remove ice cream from pan, beat in large bowl with electric mixer until smooth, return mixture to pan, cover, freeze overnight. Serve with tuiles.

Macadamia Tuiles: Beat egg white in small bowl with electric mixer until soft peaks form, gradually add sugar, beat until dissolved. Fold in sifted flour, cooled butter and essence. Place level teaspoons of mixture about 10cm apart on well greased oven tray. Cook only 4 at a time. Use back of teaspoon to spread mixture evenly to about 6cm rounds. Sprinkle with nuts.

Bake in moderate oven for about 4 minutes or until edges are set. Lift tuiles carefully from tray with spatula, place over rolling pin to curl; cool. Repeat with remaining mixture.

Serves 6.

WALNUT GINGERBREAD ICE CREAM

Ice cream can be made 3 days ahead; keep, covered, in freezer. This recipe is not suitable to microwave.

4 egg yolks
⅓ cup castor sugar
1⅓ cups milk
⅔ cup thickened cream
WALNUT GINGERBREAD
¼ cup golden syrup
¼ cup milk
2 tablespoons brown sugar
60g butter
¾ cup plain flour
¼ teaspoon bicarbonate of soda
1 tablespoon ground ginger
1 teaspoon ground cinnamon
¼ cup chopped walnuts
1 egg, lightly beaten

Beat egg yolks and sugar in small bowl with electric mixer until thick and creamy. Combine milk and cream in small saucepan, bring to boil, remove from heat. Gradually beat hot milk mixture into egg yolk mixture, beat until thick; cool. Pour mixture into lamington pan, cover, freeze until firm.

Remove ice cream from pan, beat in large bowl with electric mixer until smooth, fold in crumbled gingerbread, return mixture to pan, cover, freeze for several hours or until firm.

Walnut Gingerbread: Grease 19cm x 29cm lamington pan, cover base with paper, grease paper.

Combine golden syrup, milk, sugar and butter in medium saucepan, stir over heat, without boiling, until butter is melted and sugar dissolved. Bring to boil, remove from heat, cool to room temperature.

Stir in sifted dry ingredients and nuts in 2 batches, stir in egg. Pour mixture into prepared pan. Bake in moderate oven for about 20 minutes or until firm. Stand for 5 minutes before turning onto wire rack to cool.

Serves 6 to 8.

LEFT: From top: Walnut Gingerbread Ice Cream, Cardamom Ice Cream with Macadamia Tuiles.

Left: Glasses from The Australian East India Co.

FROZEN CASSATA BOMBE

Curacao Triple Sec is an orange-flavoured liqueur. Bombe can be made 3 days ahead; keep, covered, in freezer. This recipe is not suitable to microwave.

**¼ cup chopped glacé cherries
¼ cup chopped glacé pineapple
¼ cup chopped glacé apricots
¼ cup chopped sultanas
1 tablespoon chopped mixed peel
1 tablespoon Curacao Triple Sec
5 egg yolks
⅓ cup castor sugar
2 teaspoons vanilla essence
1¾ cups thickened cream
75g dark chocolate, melted
¼ cup packaged ground almonds**

Line pudding steamer (5 cup capacity) with plastic wrap. Combine fruit and liqueur in small bowl, mix well, cover, stand 3 hours.

Beat egg yolks and sugar in top of double saucepan (or large heatproof bowl) over simmering water until thick and creamy, remove from heat. Beat essence and cream in small bowl until soft peaks form, fold into egg yolk mixture in 2 batches. Pour two-thirds of mixture into lamington pan, cover, freeze for several hours or until firm.

Combine remaining mixture with chocolate, pour into prepared steamer, cover, freeze until firm.

Remove half of frozen plain mixture from pan, beat in small bowl with electric mixer until smooth, stir in fruit mixture. Pour mixture into steamer, cover, freeze.

Beat remaining plain mixture in small bowl with electric mixer until smooth, stir in almonds. Pour mixture into steamer, cover, freeze overnight. Turn bombe onto plate, peel away plastic wrap, cut into wedges to serve.

ABOVE: Frozen Cassata Bombe.

Above: Stand from Empire Studios

STRAWBERRY PARFAIT

Dessert can be made 2 days ahead; keep, covered, in freezer. This recipe is not suitable to microwave.

½ cup castor sugar
⅓ cup water
4 egg yolks
300ml carton thickened cream
½ x 250g punnet strawberries
red food colouring

Place strip of foil to cover base and extend over 2 opposite ends of 8cm x 26cm bar pan.

Combine sugar and water in small saucepan, stir over heat, without boiling, until sugar is dissolved, bring to boil, boil, uncovered, for 5 minutes, without stirring, remove from heat.

Beat egg yolks in small heatproof bowl with electric mixer until thick and creamy, gradually beat in hot sugar syrup, beat until mixture is cool, pour mixture into large bowl. Beat cream in small bowl until soft peaks form, fold into egg yolk mixture.

Blend or process strawberries until smooth; strain. Fold strawberries into egg yolk mixture; tint with colouring, if desired. Pour mixture into prepared pan, cover with foil, freeze overnight.

Serves 4.

MARASCHINO ICE CREAM CAKE WITH STRAWBERRY COULIS

Maraschino is a cherry-flavoured liqueur. Cake can be made 3 days ahead; keep, covered, in freezer. Recipe unsuitable to microwave.

200g packet coconut macaroons, crushed
250g packet plain sweet biscuits, crushed
180g unsalted butter, melted
2 tablespoons Maraschino
MARASCHINO CUSTARD
6 egg yolks
⅓ cup castor sugar
⅓ cup Maraschino
2 x 300ml cartons thickened cream
STRAWBERRY COULIS
250g punnet strawberries
1 tablespoon icing sugar

Grease 22cm springform tin, line base with foil, grease foil. Combine macaroons, biscuits, butter and liqueur in large bowl. Press one-third of mixture into prepared tin. Pour one-third of custard into tin, cover, freeze until firm.

Repeat layering with remaining crumb mixture and custard, freezing until firm between layers, ending with custard. Remove cake from tin, serve with strawberry coulis.

Maraschino Custard: Beat yolks, sugar and liqueur in small bowl with electric mixer until thick and creamy. Place egg yolk mixture in top of double saucepan (or heatproof bowl), beat over simmering water until mixture thickens slightly. Transfer mixture to large bowl, cover, cool to room temperature. Beat cream in small bowl until soft peaks form, fold into egg yolk mixture.

Strawberry Coulis: Blend or process strawberries and sugar until smooth.

Serves 8.

ABOVE: From left: Maraschino Ice Cream Cake with Strawberry Coulis, Strawberry Parfait.

Above: China from Orrefors

LICORICE ICE CREAM

We used Callard & Bowser toffees in this recipe. Ice cream can be made 3 days ahead; keep, covered, in freezer. Recipe unsuitable to microwave.

3 x 50g packets licorice toffees
1 cup milk
300ml carton thickened cream
2 tablespoons castor sugar
4 egg yolks

Combine toffees, milk and cream in medium saucepan, stir over heat, without boiling, until toffees have dissolved, bring to boil, remove from heat. Beat sugar and egg yolks in small bowl with electric mixer until thick and creamy. Beat hot milk mixture gradually into egg yolk mixture; cool.

Pour mixture into deep cake pan, cover, freeze until firm.

Remove ice cream from pan, beat in large bowl with electric mixer until smooth, return mixture to pan, cover, freeze until firm.

Serves 6.

PEACH TORTONI

Cointreau is an orange-flavoured liqueur. Tortoni can be made 2 days ahead; keep, covered, in freezer.

1 cup (125g) slivered almonds
300ml carton thickened cream
⅓ cup chopped glacé peaches
1 cup (60g) crushed vanilla cream wafer biscuits
1 tablespoon Cointreau
2 egg whites
2 tablespoons castor sugar

Toast almonds on oven tray in moderate oven for about 5 minutes.

Beat cream in small bowl until soft peaks form, fold in almonds, peaches, wafer crumbs and liqueur. Beat egg whites in small bowl with electric mixer until firm peaks form, gradually add sugar, beat until sugar is dissolved. Lightly fold meringue mixture into cream mixture. Spoon mixture into 6 dishes (¾ cup capacity), cover, freeze until firm.

Serves 6.

LEFT: Licorice Ice Cream.
RIGHT: From top: Peach Tortoni, Butterscotch Rum Moulds.

Left: Glasses from The Australian East India Co.

BUTTERSCOTCH RUM MOULDS

Desserts are best made a day ahead; keep, covered, in freezer. This recipe is not suitable to microwave.

½ cup brown sugar
60g butter
½ cup water
3 egg yolks
1 tablespoon underproof dark rum
300ml carton thickened cream

Combine sugar, butter and water in medium saucepan, stir over heat, without boiling, until butter has melted and sugar is dissolved. Bring to boil, reduce heat, simmer, uncovered, for 5 minutes; without stirring, remove from heat, stand for 10 minutes.

Beat egg yolks in small bowl with electric mixer until thick and creamy. Gradually beat in hot sugar syrup, in a thin stream; stir in rum. Return mixture to pan, stir over heat, without boiling, until custard thickens slightly.

Beat custard in large bowl with electric mixer for about 10 minutes or until cooled to room temperature. Beat cream in small bowl until soft peaks form, fold into custard mixture.

Pour mixture into 6 moulds (⅓ cup capacity) cover, freeze until firm. Turn desserts onto plates. Serve with fruit, if desired.

Serves 6.

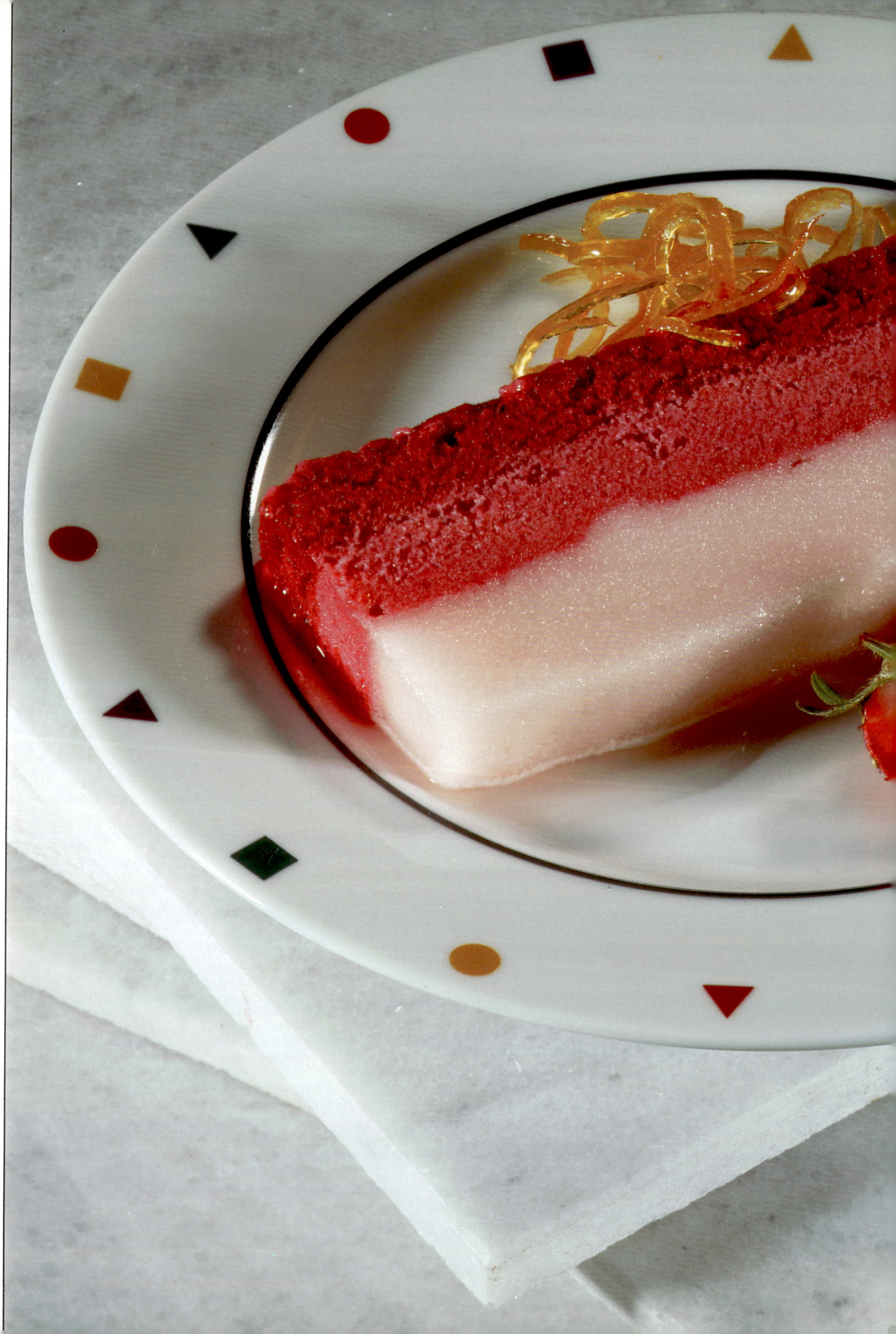

LAYERED PINK SORBET TERRINE

Terrine can be made 3 days ahead; keep, covered in freezer. This recipe is not suitable to microwave.

¾ cup castor sugar
1 cup water
⅔ cup pink champagne
⅔ cup strained fresh lemon juice
red food colouring
2 egg whites
RASPBERRY SORBET
½ cup castor sugar
1 cup water
200g fresh or frozen raspberries
1 egg white
BOYSENBERRY SORBET
½ cup sugar
1 cup water
200g fresh or frozen boysenberries
1 egg white

Line base and sides of 15cm x 25cm loaf pan with foil.

Combine sugar and water in medium saucepan, stir over heat, without boiling, until sugar is dissolved. Bring to boil, boil, uncovered, for 8 minutes, without stirring; cool to room temperature.

Stir in champagne and lemon juice; tint with colouring, if desired. Pour mixture into lamington pan, cover, freeze until partly set. Process egg whites with champagne mixture until smooth. Pour mixture into prepared loaf pan, cover, freeze until firm.

Spread raspberry sorbet over frozen champagne sorbet, cover, freeze until firm.

Spread boysenberry sorbet over frozen raspberry sorbet, cover, freeze until firm.

Turn terrine out just before serving.
Raspberry Sorbet: Combine sugar and water in small saucepan, stir over heat, without boiling, until sugar is dissolved. Bring to boil, boil, uncovered, for 5 minutes, without stirring; cool to room temperature.

Blend or process berries and sugar syrup until smooth, strain. Pour mixture into lamington pan, cover, freeze until partly set. Process egg white with berry mixture until smooth.
Boysenberry Sorbet: Follow method given for raspberry sorbet.

Serves 8.

LEFT: Layered Pink Sorbet Terrine.

Left: Plate from Dansab.

MERINGUE KISSES WITH PASSIONFRUIT GLAZE

You will need about 10 passionfruit for this recipe. Meringues can be made a week ahead; keep in airtight container. Passionfruit butter can be made 2 weeks ahead; keep, covered, in refrigerator. This recipe is not suitable to freeze or microwave.

2 egg whites
½ cup castor sugar
PASSIONFRUIT BUTTER
2 egg yolks
½ cup castor sugar
¼ cup passionfruit pulp
1 tablespoon water
60g butter
PASSIONFRUIT GLAZE
¼ cup castor sugar
½ cup passionfruit pulp

Lightly grease 2 oven trays, cover with paper. Using a 2cm round cutter, mark 16 circles on paper.

Beat egg whites in small bowl with electric mixer until soft peaks form, gradually beat in sugar, beat until dissolved between additions. Spoon mixture into large piping bag fitted with small fluted tube. Pipe 3cm high rosettes of mixture onto paper. Bake in very slow oven for about 30 minutes or until meringues are dry to touch. Cool in oven with door ajar. Sandwich meringues with passionfruit butter. Serve with glaze.

Passionfruit Butter: Combine egg yolks, sugar, passionfruit, water and butter in top of double saucepan (or in heatproof bowl), stir over simmering water until mixture thickens and coats back of spoon; cool to room temperature.

Passionfruit Glaze: Combine sugar and passionfruit in small saucepan, stir over medium heat, without boiling, until sugar is dissolved; strain, cool.

Serves 6.

RIGHT: Meringue Kisses with Passionfruit Glaze.
BELOW: Peachy Ice Cream Swans.

Right: China from Studio-Haus. Below: Cover plate from Made Where; column from Mid City Home and Garden

PEACHY ICE CREAM SWANS

We used Seagram's peach liqueur in this recipe. Ice cream can be made 2 weeks ahead; keep, covered, in freezer. Meringues can be made 2 days ahead; keep in airtight container. Sauce can be made a day ahead; keep, covered, in refrigerator. This recipe is not suitable to microwave.

3 egg whites
¾ cup castor sugar
PEACH SAUCE
2 teaspoons cornflour
250ml bottle peach nectar
2 teaspoons castor sugar
2 tablespoons peach liqueur
PEACH ICE CREAM
3 medium peaches
¼ cup milk
300ml carton thickened cream
5 egg yolks
⅓ cup castor sugar

Lightly grease 2 large oven trays, cover with paper. Mark 16 large teardrop shapes on paper about 7cm in length, and 16 smaller teardrop shapes about 4cm in length.

Beat egg whites in small bowl with electric mixer until soft peaks form; gradually add sugar, beat until dissolved between additions. Spoon two-thirds of meringue into large piping bag fitted with a 1cm plain tube, pipe mixture over shapes marked on paper until about 1cm thick. Spoon remaining mixture into another piping bag fitted with a 5mm plain tube, pipe 8 necks about 5cm in length for large swans. Pipe 8 necks about 3cm in length for small swans.

Bake meringues in very slow oven for approximately 1 hour or until meringues are firm to touch. Cool in oven with door ajar. When meringues are cold, carefully remove from trays.

Pour sauce onto plates, place a large and small scoop of ice cream onto sauce, gently press meringue wings and necks into ice cream.

Peach Sauce: Blend cornflour with 1 tablespoon of the nectar in small saucepan, stir in remaining nectar and sugar. Stir over high heat until mixture boils and thickens, cool to room temperature; stir in liqueur.

Peach Ice Cream: Blend or process peaches until smooth. Combine milk and cream in small saucepan, bring to boil, remove from heat. Beat egg yolks and sugar in medium bowl with electric mixer until thick and creamy, beat in peach purée. Gradually beat in hot milk mixture while motor is operating; cool. Pour mixture into shallow freezer trays, cover, freeze several hours or until firm. Remove ice cream from trays, beat in large bowl with electric mixer until thick; return mixture to trays, cover, freeze until firm.

Serves 8

MOCHA MERINGUE TRIANGLES

Kahlua is a coffee-flavoured liqueur. Unfilled meringues can be made 3 days ahead; keep in airtight container. Filling can be made 2 days ahead; keep, covered, in refrigerator. Recipe unsuitable to freeze or microwave.

1 tablespoon flaked almonds
2 egg whites
½ cup castor sugar
30g dark chocolate, melted
1 teaspoon oil
MOCHA FILLING
¼ cup thickened cream
½ teaspoon dry instant coffee
90g dark chocolate, chopped
¼ cup sour cream
2 teaspoons Kahlua

Toast almonds on oven tray in moderate oven for about 5 minutes. Lightly grease 2 oven trays, cover with paper; grease paper. Mark 16 x 6cm triangles on paper.

Beat egg whites in small bowl with electric mixer until soft peaks form. Gradually add sugar, beat until dissolved between additions. Spoon mixture into large piping bag fitted with 5mm plain tube. Pipe mixture evenly over triangles marked on trays, sprinkle 4 meringues with almonds. Bake in very slow oven for about 1½ hours or until dry to touch. Cool in oven with door ajar.

Combine chocolate and oil in small bowl. Spread tops of 4 meringues with chocolate, allow to set. Spread filling over plain meringues, top half with almond meringues and half with chocolate meringues.

Mocha Filling: Heat cream and coffee in small saucepan, bring to boil. Remove from heat, add chocolate, stir until melted. Stir in sour cream and liqueur; transfer to small bowl, cover, refrigerate for 1 hour. Beat with electric mixer for about 30 seconds or until just thick; do not overbeat.

Serves 4.

ABOVE: Mocha Meringue Triangles.

Plate from Mikasa.

TANGERINE MERINGUE CUPS

You will need to buy about 6 tangerines for this recipe. Grand Marnier is an orange-flavoured liqueur. Meringue cups can be made 3 days ahead; keep in airtight container. This recipe is not suitable to freeze or microwave.

¼ cup flaked almonds
3 egg whites
¾ cup castor sugar
150g dark chocolate, melted
2 teaspoons oil
4 medium tangerines
vanilla ice cream
SYRUP
1 tablespoon castor sugar
2 tablespoons tangerine juice
2 tablespoons Grand Marnier
1 tablespoon thinly sliced glacé ginger

Toast almonds on oven tray in moderate oven for about 5 minutes; cool, crush lightly. Cover oven tray with paper, lightly grease and flour paper. Cover outside of 4 round moulds (⅓ cup capacity) with foil, trim edges. Place moulds upside down on tray.

Beat egg whites in small bowl with electric mixer until soft peaks form, gradually add sugar, beat until dissolved between additions. Spoon mixture into large piping bag fitted with 1cm plain tube. Starting from base of each mould, pipe meringue evenly around sides until moulds are covered. Bake in very slow oven for about 1 hour or until meringues are firm to touch. Cool in oven with door ajar. Carefully remove mould and foil from meringue cups.

Combine chocolate and oil in small bowl, mix well, brush inside and top edge of each meringue cup with chocolate mixture. Dip into almonds. Remove skin and pith from tangerines, cut into segments, reserve any juice for syrup. Combine segments and syrup in small bowl, stand for 30 minutes. Place a scoop of ice cream into each meringue cup, serve with segments and syrup, decorate with shredded tangerine rind, if desired.

Syrup: Combine sugar and juice in small saucepan, stir over heat, without boiling, until sugar is dissolved. Bring to boil, remove from heat; cool. Stir in liqueur and ginger.

Serves 4.

CHOCOLATE HAZELNUT MERINGUE

Recipe is best made a day ahead; keep, covered, in refrigerator. Recipe unsuitable to freeze or microwave.

5 egg whites
¾ cup castor sugar
1 teaspoon vanilla essence
½ cup packaged ground hazelnuts
¼ cup icing sugar
1 tablespoon cornflour
250g white chocolate, melted
FILLING
300ml carton thickened cream
1 teaspoon vanilla essence
¼ cup underproof dark rum
300g milk chocolate, melted

Lightly grease 3 x 23cm springform tins, cover bases with paper, grease paper. Beat egg whites in medium bowl with electric mixer until firm peaks form; gradually add sugar, beat until dissolved between additions. Stir in essence and hazelnuts. Fold in sifted dry ingredients. Divide mixture between prepared tins, spread evenly over bases. Bake in moderate oven for 10 minutes or until firm and lightly browned, turn onto wire racks to cool. Spread each layer with white chocolate. Sandwich layers with two-thirds of the filling. Cover and decorate with remaining filling.
Filling: Beat cream, essence and rum in small bowl until soft peaks form. Stir in cooled chocolate; refrigerate for 2 hours before using.

CLASSIC PAVLOVA

Pavlova can be made a week ahead; keep in airtight container. Fill pavlova an hour before serving. This recipe unsuitable to freeze or microwave.

4 egg whites
1 cup castor sugar
1 tablespoon cornflour
1 teaspoon lemon juice
300ml carton thickened cream
1 tablespoon icing sugar
1 medium orange, segmented
1 medium banana, sliced
6 strawberries
2 medium passionfruit

Cover oven tray with foil, grease foil, dust with flour, mark a 23cm diameter circle on foil.
Beat egg whites in small bowl with electric mixer until soft peaks form, gradually add sugar, beat until sugar is dissolved between additions. Fold in cornflour and juice. Spread quarter of mixture over circle leaving a 3cm border. Spoon remaining mixture into a large piping bag fitted with fluted tube. Pipe a thick border around meringue circle to form a shell. Bake in very slow oven for about 1½ hours or until meringue is dry and firm to touch. Cool in oven with door ajar.
Beat cream and sifted icing sugar in small bowl, until firm peaks form; fill meringue shell with cream; decorate with fruit.

LEFT: Tangerine Meringue Cups.
ABOVE: From top: Classic Pavlova, Chocolate Hazelnut Meringue.

Left: Plate and fabric from Decorator Blinds. Above: Table from Country Form; plates from The Bay Tree; cake tin from Sydney Antique Centre.

MARBLED STRAWBERRY BOMBE

Cakes can be made 2 days ahead; keep in airtight container or freeze for 2 months. Bombe is best assembled on day of serving; keep, covered, in freezer. Cover with meringue just before baking. This recipe is not suitable to microwave.

4 eggs
¾ cup castor sugar
⅔ cup plain flour
⅓ cup self-raising flour
⅓ cup cornflour
red food colouring
1 tablespoon cocoa
15g butter, melted
½ cup port
2 x 420g cans strawberries, drained
1 litre strawberry ripple ice cream
6 egg whites
1½ cups castor sugar, extra

Lightly grease 2 deep 20cm round cake pans, cover bases with paper, grease paper.

Beat whole eggs in small bowl with electric mixer until thick and creamy. Gradually add sugar, beat until dissolved between additions. Transfer mixture to large bowl. Gently fold in sifted flours in 2 batches. Divide mixture between 3 bowls. Tint 1 bowl of mixture with red colouring. Blend sifted cocoa with butter, stir into second bowl of mixture. Leave third bowl of mixture plain. Spoon the 3 mixtures alternately into prepared pans, pull skewer through mixtures to give marbled effect.

Bake in moderate oven for about 25 minutes or until firm. Stand 5 minutes before turning onto wire racks to cool. When cold, sprinkle cakes with port, place 1 cake on heatproof plate, arrange strawberries over cake, top with remaining cake. Soften ice cream slightly, spoon onto cake, shape into a dome, cover, freeze until firm.

Beat egg whites in medium bowl with electric mixer until soft peaks form, gradually add extra sugar, beat until dissolved between additions. Spoon mixture into large piping bag fitted with plain tube. Starting from base of cake, pipe mixture evenly around cake and ice cream until completely covered. Bake in hot oven for about 3 minutes or until meringue is lightly browned. Serve immediately.

RIGHT: From top: Marbled Strawberry Bombe, Meringue Terrine with Chocolate Sauce.

Plates from Mikasa; stone urns from Parterre Garden; roses from Whitehouse Interior Design

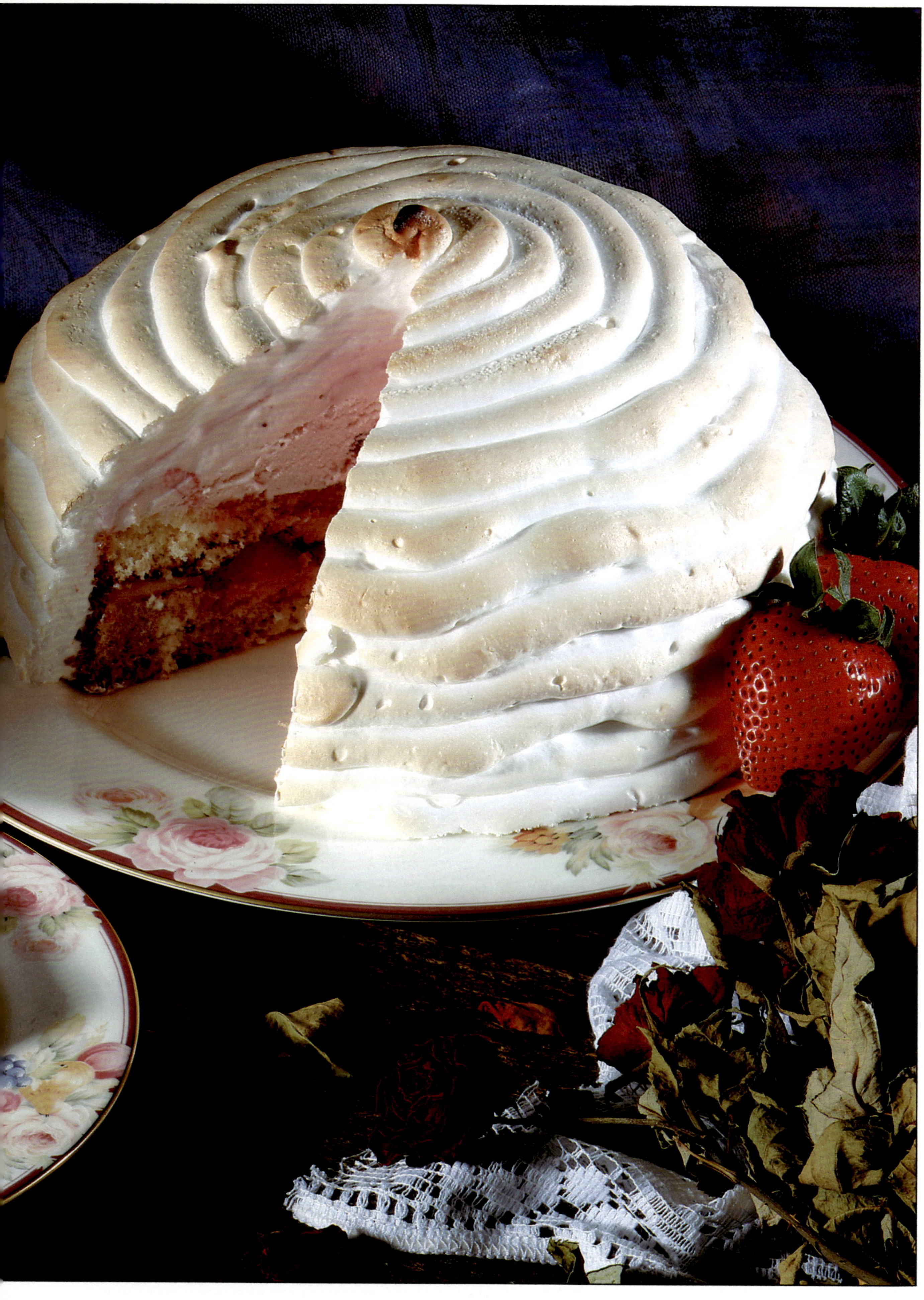

MERINGUE TERRINE WITH CHOCOLATE SAUCE

Kahlua is a coffee-flavoured liqueur. Terrine is best made up to about 6 hours before serving. This recipe is not suitable to freeze or microwave.

4 egg whites
½ cup castor sugar
FILLING
300ml carton thickened cream
1 tablespoon dry instant coffee
1 tablespoon Kahlua
CHOCOLATE SAUCE
150g dark chocolate, melted
¾ cup cream
2 teaspoons Kahlua

Lightly grease a 25cm x 30cm Swiss roll pan, cover base with paper, grease paper; dust with cornflour, shake away excess cornflour.

Beat egg whites in small bowl with electric mixer until soft peaks form, gradually add sugar, beat until sugar is dissolved between additions. Spread mixture evenly into prepared pan. Bake in moderate oven for about 10 minutes or until meringue is firm to touch. Remove from oven, turn onto sheet of paper, carefully remove paper from base, cool to room temperature. Cut meringue into 3 pieces. Sandwich pieces of meringue with half the filling. Cover and decorate terrine with remaining filling. Serve sliced with chocolate sauce.

Filling: Beat cream, coffee and liqueur in small bowl until firm peaks form.

Chocolate Sauce: Combine chocolate, cream and liqueur in small bowl, stir until smooth.

PASSIONFRUIT GINGER CHEESECAKE

You will need about 8 passionfruit and 2 mangoes for this recipe. Grand Marnier is an orange-flavoured liqueur. Cheesecake is best made a day ahead; keep, covered, in refrigerator. This recipe is not suitable to freeze or microwave.

4 eggs
⅔ cup castor sugar
⅓ cup cornflour
⅓ cup plain flour
⅓ cup self-raising flour
SYRUP
½ cup castor sugar
1 cup water
1 tablespoon green ginger wine
FILLING
250g packet cream cheese, softened
400g can sweetened condensed milk
¾ cup passionfruit pulp
1 tablespoon green ginger wine
1 tablespoon chopped glacé ginger
½ cup sour cream
1 tablespoon gelatine
¼ cup water
MANGO SAUCE
2 tablespoons strained passionfruit pulp
1 cup mango purée
1 tablespoon castor sugar
½ cup orange juice
2 tablespoons Grand Marnier

Grease deep 23cm round cake pan, cover base with paper; grease paper.

Beat eggs in small bowl with electric mixer until thick and creamy. Gradually add sugar, beat until sugar is dissolved between additions. Transfer to large bowl, gently fold in sifted flours. Spread mixture evenly into prepared pan. Bake in moderate oven for about 40 minutes or until sponge is firm. Turn onto wire rack to cool.

With sponge right way up, gently scoop out centre, leaving 1cm shell. Cake crumbs can be frozen for use in another recipe. Line the same cake pan with plastic wrap, place cake shell in pan, brush inside of sponge with warm syrup. Pour filling into sponge, refrigerate until set. Decorate with whipped cream and extra passionfruit pulp, if desired. Serve with sauce.

Syrup: Combine sugar and water in small saucepan, stir over heat, without boiling, until sugar is dissolved. Bring to boil, boil, uncovered, without stirring, for about 4 minutes or until reduced by half. Stir in ginger wine.

Filling: Beat cheese in medium bowl with electric mixer until smooth. Stir in milk, passionfruit, wine, ginger and sour cream. Sprinkle gelatine over water in small bowl, stand in small pan of simmering water, stir until dissolved (or microwave on HIGH for about 30 seconds). Cool to room temperature; do not allow to set. Stir into passionfruit mixture.

Mango Sauce: Blend or process all ingredients until smooth.

BAKED LEMON SOUR CREAM CHEESECAKE

Cheesecake can be made 3 days ahead; keep, covered, in refrigerator. This recipe is not suitable to freeze or microwave.

2 cups (250g) plain sweet biscuit crumbs
125g unsalted butter, melted
FILLING
250g packet cream cheese, softened
250g carton low-fat cottage cheese
3 eggs
¾ cup castor sugar
2 tablespoons cornflour
300g carton sour cream
2 teaspoons grated lemon rind
¼ cup lemon juice

Lightly grease 20cm springform tin, cover base with foil, grease foil.

Combine crumbs and butter in small bowl, mix well; press mixture over base and side of prepared tin, refrigerate until firm. Pour filling into crust, stand tin on oven tray. Bake in moderately slow oven for about 1 hour or until just firm in centre; cool in oven with door ajar. Refrigerate several hours or overnight. Decorate with whipped cream and ground nutmeg, if desired.

Filling: Beat cheeses in medium bowl with electric mixer until well combined. Add eggs, 1 at a time, beating well after each addition. Beat in sugar and cornflour, then cream, rind and juice.

RIGHT: From top: Passionfruit Ginger Cheesecake, Baked Lemon Sour Cream Cheesecake.

Right: Trays from Un Jardin... En Plus

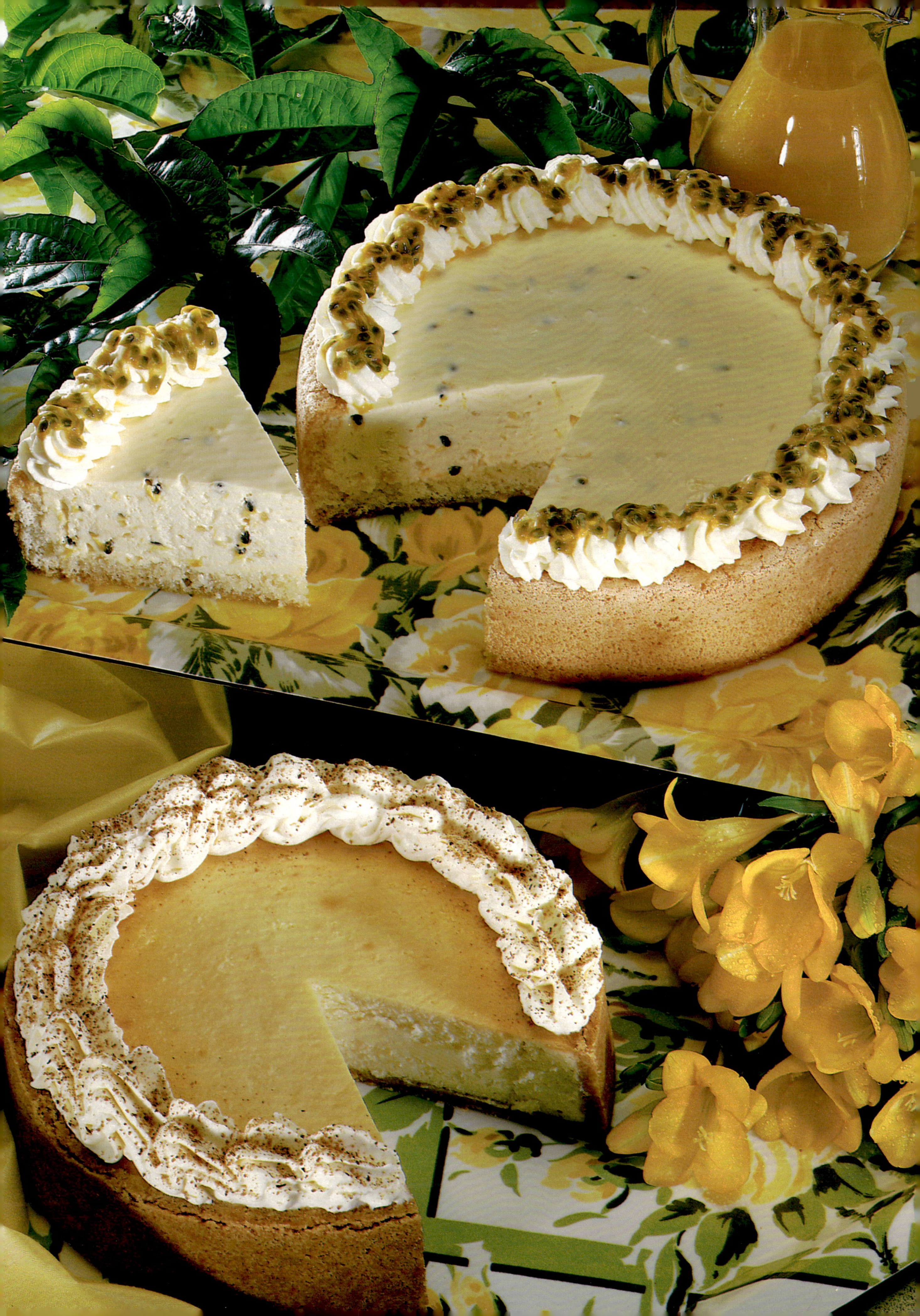

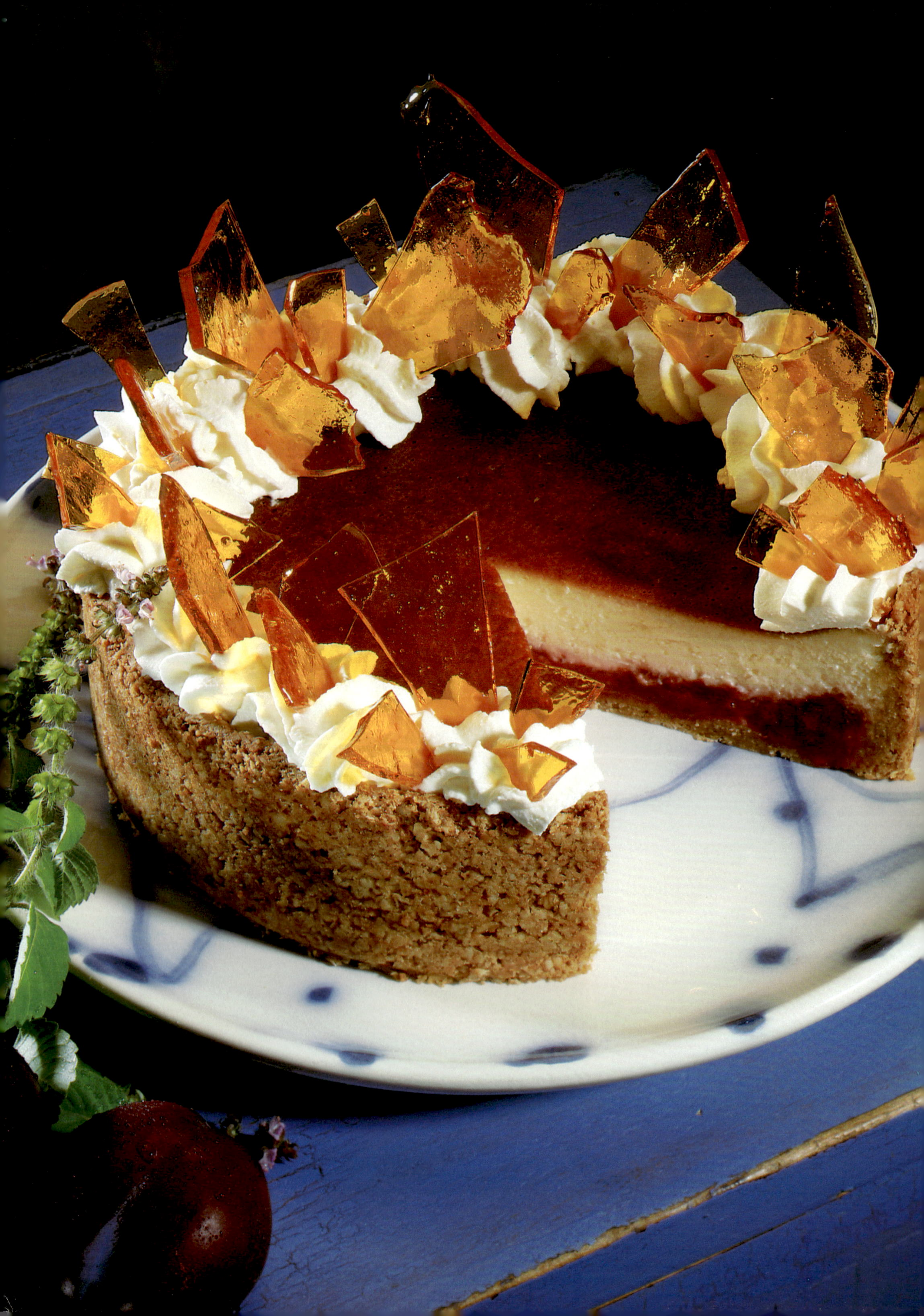

PLUM CHEESECAKE WITH TOFFEE

Cheesecake can be made a day ahead; keep, covered, in refrigerator. Recipe unsuitable to freeze or microwave.

150g butter, melted
3 cups rolled oats
⅓ cup brown sugar
FILLING
500g blood plums, chopped
1 tablespoon water
⅓ cup castor sugar
2 tablespoons lemon juice
125g packet cream cheese, softened
½ cup castor sugar, extra
3 eggs
300ml carton thickened cream
TOPPING
¾ cup castor sugar
⅓ cup water
300ml carton thickened cream

Combine butter, oats and sugar in medium bowl; mix well. Press evenly over base and side of 23cm springform tin. Refrigerate for 30 minutes. Pour plum mixture into crust, carefully top with cheese mixture. Stand tin on oven tray. Bake in moderately slow oven for about 1 hour or until set. Cool in oven with door ajar; refrigerate for several hours. Decorate with whipped cream and toffee.

Filling: Combine plums, water, sugar and half the juice in large saucepan, bring to boil, reduce heat, cover, simmer for about 10 minutes or until plums are soft. Stir mixture over heat for about 10 minutes or until thick; cool to room temperature. Beat cheese, extra sugar and remaining juice in small bowl with electric mixer until smooth. Beat in eggs, 1 at a time. Stir in cream.

Topping: Combine sugar and water in small saucepan, stir over heat, without boiling, until sugar is dissolved. Bring to boil, boil, uncovered, without stirring, for about 8 minutes or until mixture turns a light golden colour. Pour mixture onto foil-covered tray, leave to set. Break toffee into pieces. Beat cream in small bowl until firm peaks form.

CUMQUAT LIQUEUR CHEESECAKE

Grand Marnier is an orange-flavoured liqueur. You will need about 300g fresh cumquats for this recipe. We used Butter Nut biscuits in the base. Cheesecake can be made a day ahead, keep, covered, in refrigerator. This recipe is not suitable to freeze.

1 cup plain sweet biscuit crumbs
60g butter, melted
2 tablespoons finely chopped walnuts or pecans
FILLING
¼ cup cumquat juice
1 tablespoon lemon juice
2 teaspoons finely chopped cumquat rind
250g packet cream cheese, softened
½ cup sweetened condensed milk
½ cup brown sugar
⅓ cup Grand Marnier
2 tablespoons gelatine
⅓ cup water
TOPPING
2 cups water
4 large cumquats, thinly sliced
¼ cup brown sugar
¼ cup castor sugar
2 tablespoons Grand Marnier
1½ tablespoons gelatine
¼ cup water, extra

Combine crumbs, butter and nuts in medium bowl; mix well. Press evenly over base of 23cm springform tin, refrigerate until firm. Pour filling over base, refrigerate several hours or until firm. Carefully pour cooled topping over filling, refrigerate until firm.

Filling: Combine juices and rind in small saucepan, (reserve remaining squeezed cumquats for topping). Bring to boil, boil, uncovered, for about 3 minutes or until mixture is reduced to about 1 tablespoon; cool. Beat cheese, milk, sugar and liqueur in large bowl with electric mixer until smooth, stir in juice mixture. Sprinkle gelatine over water in small bowl, stand in small pan of simmering water, stir until dissolved, (or microwave on HIGH for 30 seconds). Cool to room temperature; do not allow to set. Stir gelatine mixture into cheese mixture.

Topping: Combine reserved cumquats and water in small saucepan, bring to boil, boil, uncovered, for about 5 minutes or until liquid is reduced to about 1½ cups; strain, discard cumquats. Stir in sliced cumquats, sugars and liqueur. Stir over heat, without boiling, until sugars have dissolved, bring to boil, reduce heat, simmer, uncovered, without stirring, for 2 minutes; cool.

Sprinkle gelatine over extra water in small bowl, stand in small pan of simmering water, stir until dissolved, (or microwave on HIGH for about 30 seconds), cool to room temperature. Do not allow to set. Stir gelatine mixture into cooled syrup.

LEFT: Plum Cheesecake with Toffee.
BELOW: Cumquat Liqueur Cheesecake.

Left: Plate from Mid City Home and Garden; cupboard from Country Form. Below: Glass plate from Studio-Haus; tray from The Country Trader

CHOCOLATE RUM CHEESECAKE

Cheesecake can be made a day ahead; keep, covered, in refrigerator. This recipe is not suitable to freeze or microwave.

2 eggs
⅓ cup castor sugar
2 tablespoons plain flour
2 tablespoons self-raising flour
2 tablespoons cornflour
2 tablespoons underproof dark rum
300ml carton thickened cream
100g dark chocolate, grated
FILLING
1 egg
⅓ cup castor sugar
250g packet cream cheese, softened
3 teaspoons gelatine
2 tablespoons water
300ml carton thickened cream
1 tablespoon underproof dark rum
60g dark chocolate, melted
2 teaspoons vanilla essence

Grease 20cm springform tin, cover base with paper, grease paper.
Beat eggs in small bowl with electric mixer until thick and creamy. Gradually add sugar, beat until dissolved between additions. Gently fold in sifted flours, spread mixture into prepared tin. Bake in moderate oven for about 20 minutes or until firm. Turn sponge onto wire rack to cool.
Cut cold sponge into 2 layers. Return 1 layer to springform tin, brush with half the rum. Pour chocolate mixture over sponge, refrigerate until set. Carefully pour vanilla mixture over chocolate layer. Brush 1 side of remaining sponge layer with remaining rum, place over vanilla layer, rum side down, refrigerate until firm. Beat cream until soft peaks form. Cover cake with two-thirds of the cream, press chocolate around side of cake. Decorate with remaining cream and chocolate curls, if desired.
Filling: Beat egg and sugar in small bowl with electric mixer until thick and creamy. Gradually beat in cheese, beat until smooth. Sprinkle gelatine over water in small bowl, stand in small pan of simmering water, stir until dissolved (or microwave on HIGH for about 20 seconds). Stir gelatine mixture into cheese mixture. Beat cream until soft peaks form, fold into cheese mixture. Divide mixture evenly into 2 small bowls. Stir rum and chocolate into 1 bowl. Stir essence into remaining bowl of mixture.

JELLY CRUNCH CHEESECAKE

Cheesecake can be made a day ahead; keep, covered, in refrigerator. This recipe is not suitable to freeze.

1 cup plain chocolate biscuit crumbs
90g butter, melted
VANILLA FILLING
250g packet cream cheese, softened
1 tablespoon castor sugar
1 teaspoon grated lemon rind
1½ tablespoons lemon juice
85g packet vanilla instant pudding mix
¾ cup milk
TOPPING
2 x 250g punnets strawberries
85g packet strawberry jelly crystals
1¼ cups boiling water

Lightly oil 23cm springform tin, line base and side with plastic wrap.
   Combine biscuit crumbs and butter in medium bowl; mix well, press evenly over base of prepared tin; refrigerate while preparing filling.
   Spread filling evenly over base, refrigerate for 30 minutes or until firm. Arrange strawberries over filling. Pour jelly mixture over strawberries, refrigerate for several hours.
Vanilla Filling: Beat cheese, sugar, rind and juice in small bowl with electric mixer until smooth, beat in pudding mix. Gradually beat in milk.
Topping: Cut strawberries in half. Combine jelly crystals and water in medium bowl, stir until dissolved, cool, refrigerate until consistency of unbeaten egg whites.

LEFT: From top: Jelly Crunch Cheesecake, Chocolate Rum Cheesecake.

Left: Plates from The Country Trader

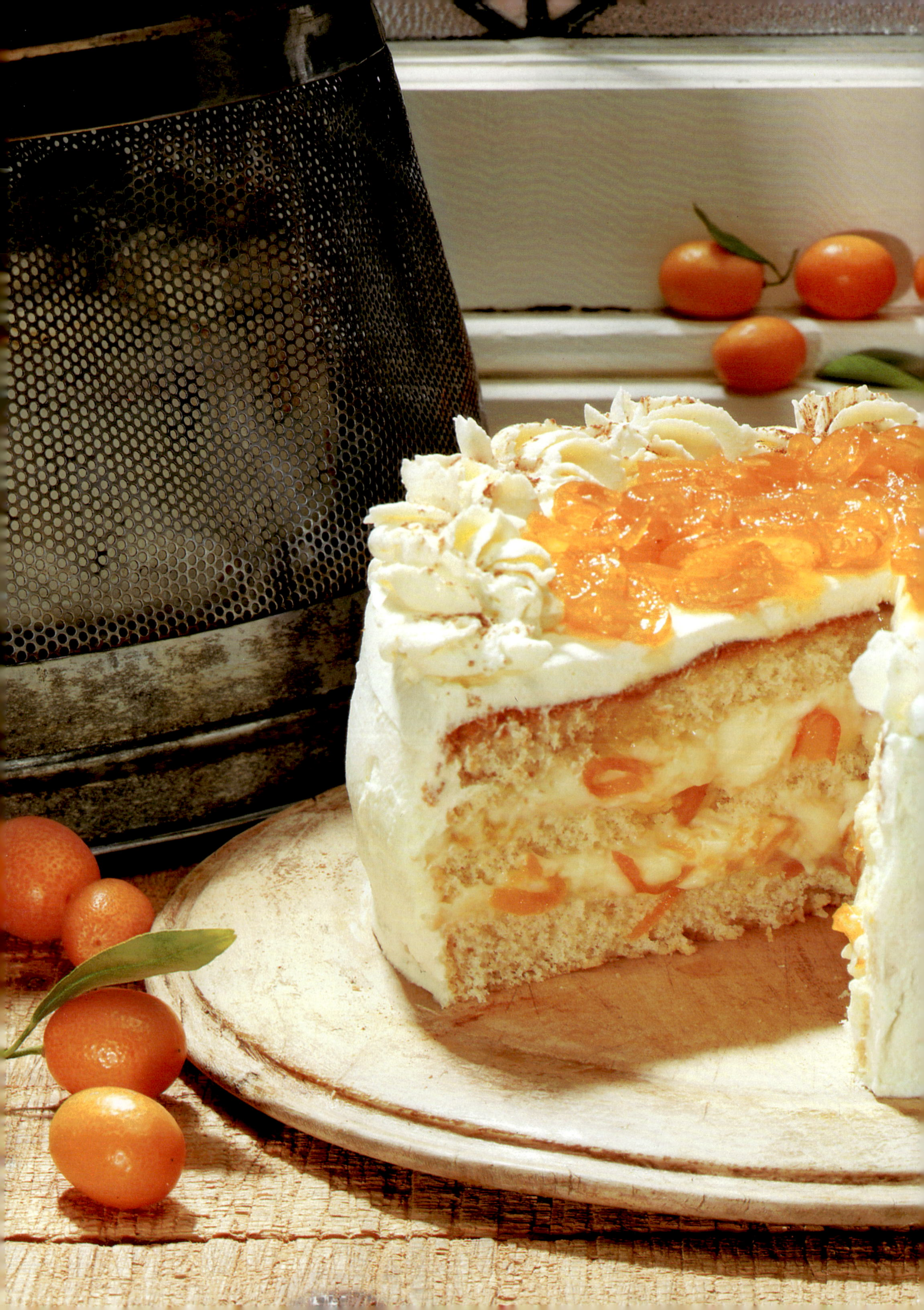

CUMQUAT LAYER CAKE

Cointreau is an orange-flavoured liqueur. Cake can be made several hours ahead; keep, covered, in refrigerator. Unfilled cake can be frozen for 2 months. This recipe is not suitable to microwave.

3 eggs
½ cup castor sugar
¼ cup plain flour
¼ cup self-raising flour
¼ cup cornflour
2 tablespoons Cointreau
300ml carton thickened cream
CUMQUAT FILLING
250g cumquats
½ cup water
½ cup castor sugar
1 tablespoon Cointreau
3 egg yolks
⅓ cup castor sugar, extra
1 tablespoon plain flour
1 tablespoon cornflour
1½ cups milk
½ cup thickened cream

Grease a deep 20cm round cake pan, cover base with paper; grease paper.

Beat eggs in small bowl with electric mixer until thick and creamy, gradually add sugar, beat until dissolved between additions. Transfer to large bowl, carefully fold in sifted flours. Spread mixture into prepared pan, bake in moderate oven for about 30 minutes or until just firm. Turn cake onto wire rack to cool. Cut cold cake into 3 layers, brush each layer with liqueur. Sandwich layers with cumquat filling. Beat cream until soft peaks form. Cover and decorate cake with cream and reserved cooked cumquats. Sprinkle with a little ground nutmeg, if desired.

Cumquat Filling: Slice unpeeled cumquats finely; discard seeds. Combine cumquats, water and sugar in medium saucepan, stir over heat, without boiling, until sugar is dissolved, bring to boil, reduce heat, simmer, uncovered, without stirring, for 5 minutes. Remove from heat, stir in liqueur; cool to room temperature.

Combine egg yolks, extra sugar and flours in medium saucepan, gradually stir in milk. Stir over high heat until mixture boils and thickens; remove from heat, cover, cool to room temperature. Beat cream in small bowl until soft peaks form, fold into custard, stir in three-quarters of cumquat mixture; reserve remaining cumquat mixture for decoration.

LEFT: Cumquat Layer Cake.

Left: Cake cover from The Country Trader

LAYERED RICOTTA CHOCOLATE CAKE

Cointreau is an orange-flavoured liqueur. Unfilled cake can be frozen for 2 months. Cake can be made a day ahead; keep, covered, in refrigerator. Recipe unsuitable to microwave.

100g unsalted butter
½ cup castor sugar
2 eggs
150g dark chocolate, melted
1½ cups self-raising flour
½ cup water
300ml carton thickened cream
¼ cup icing sugar

RICOTTA FRUIT FILLING
250g ricotta cheese
¼ cup castor sugar
1 tablespoon Cointreau
½ cup finely chopped glacé apricots
½ cup finely chopped glacé pineapple
50g dark chocolate, grated

Grease deep 25cm round cake pan, cover base with paper, grease paper.
  Beat butter and sugar in small bowl with electric mixer until light and fluffy; beat in eggs 1 at a time; stir in cooled chocolate. Transfer mixture to large bowl; fold in sifted flour and water in 2 batches. Spread mixture into prepared pan, bake in moderately slow oven for about 1 hour or until firm. Stand for 5 minutes before turning onto wire rack to cool. Cut cold cake into 3 layers, sandwich layers with filling. Beat cream and sifted icing sugar in small bowl until soft peaks form, spread over top and side of cake. Decorate with extra glacé pineapple and grated chocolate, if desired.
Ricotta Fruit Filling: Beat cheese, sugar and liqueur in small bowl with electric mixer until smooth; stir in fruit and chocolate.

COFFEE GATEAU WITH TANGERINE CREAM

You will need about 2 tangerines for this recipe. Tia Maria is a coffee-flavoured liqueur. Gateau can be made a day ahead; keep, covered, in refrigerator. Recipe unsuitable to freeze or microwave.

4 eggs, lightly beaten
½ cup castor sugar
⅔ cup plain flour
60g butter, melted
2 teaspoons dry instant coffee
¼ cup water
¼ cup Tia Maria
300ml carton thickened cream
TANGERINE CREAM
300ml carton thickened cream
1 tablespoon icing sugar
¼ cup packaged ground hazelnuts
1 tablespoon grated tangerine rind
1 tablespoon tangerine juice

Grease deep 20cm round cake pan, cover base with paper; grease paper.

Combine eggs and sugar in top of double saucepan (or heatproof bowl). Beat over simmering water with electric mixer for about 10 minutes or until thick and creamy. Transfer to large bowl, continue to beat until cooled to room temperature. Gently fold in sifted flour and cooled butter in 2 batches. Pour into prepared pan. Bake in moderate oven for about 25 minutes or until firm. Turn onto wire rack to cool.

Line the same cake pan with foil. Cut cake into 3 layers, place 1 layer into pan, sprinkle with one-third of combined coffee, water and liqueur. Top with half tangerine cream. Repeat, with remaining cake, coffee mixture and tangerine cream, finishing with a cake layer. Cover cake with foil, cover with plate slightly smaller than pan, place a weight on top, refrigerate several hours or overnight.

Turn cake onto serving plate. Beat cream in small bowl until soft peaks form. Cover and decorate cake with cream. Decorate with chocolate coated hazelnuts, tangerine rind and segments, if desired.

Tangerine Cream: Beat cream and sifted icing sugar in small bowl until soft peaks form, stir in remaining ingredients.

LEFT: Layered Ricotta Chocolate Cake.
RIGHT: Coffee Gâteau with Tangerine Cream.

Left: Fabric from Les Olivades. Right: Plate from Mikasa

COCONUT ROULADE WITH CHERRY CREAM

Kirsch is a cherry-flavoured liqueur. Recipe best made several hours before serving. This recipe is not suitable to freeze or microwave.

3 eggs
½ cup castor sugar
¼ cup coconut
¾ cup self-raising flour
¼ teaspoon coconut essence
2 tablespoons warm milk
410g can unsweetened pitted red cherries
¼ cup castor sugar, extra
2 tablespoons cornflour
1½ tablespoons water
1½ tablespoons Kirsch
½ cup cream
¼ cup water, extra

Grease 25cm x 30cm Swiss roll pan, cover base with paper; grease paper.

Beat eggs in small bowl with electric mixer until thick and creamy, gradually add sugar, beat until dissolved between additions. Transfer mixture to large bowl, fold in coconut, sifted flour, essence and milk in 2 batches. Spread mixture into prepared pan, bake in moderate oven for about 12 minutes or until firm. Turn roll onto tea-towel. Remove lining paper, roll gently from narrow end, using tea-towel to lift cake and guide roll; cool.

Combine undrained cherries and extra sugar in small saucepan, stir over heat, without boiling, until sugar is dissolved, bring to boil. Remove from heat. Blend cornflour with water in small bowl, stir into cherry mixture; stir over high heat until mixture boils and thickens; remove from heat, stir in liqueur. Cool to room temperature. Reserve one-third of cherry mixture for sauce. Gently unroll cake, spread with remaining cherry mixture, re-roll cake.

Blend or process reserved cherry mixture until smooth. Divide into 2 medium bowls. Stir cream into 1 bowl. Stir extra water into remaining bowl. Serve sliced roll with both sauces.

PECAN PUMPKIN CAKE WITH CINNAMON CREAM

Grand Marnier is an orange-flavoured liqueur. You will need to cook about 200g pumpkin for this recipe. Cake can be made a day ahead; keep, covered, in refrigerator. This recipe is not suitable to freeze or microwave.

250g butter
¾ cup castor sugar
2 eggs
½ cup chopped pecans
⅓ cup coconut
½ cup cooked mashed pumpkin
2 cups self-raising flour
½ cup milk
⅓ cup Grand Marnier
CINNAMON CREAM
2 x 300ml cartons thickened cream
1 teaspoon ground cinnamon
2 tablespoons icing sugar

Grease a deep 23cm round cake pan, cover base with paper; grease paper.

Beat butter and sugar in small bowl with electric mixer until light and fluffy. Add eggs 1 at a time, beat well between additions. Transfer mixture to large bowl, stir in nuts, coconut and pumpkin. Lightly fold in sifted flour and milk in 2 batches. Spread mixture into prepared pan. Bake in moderately slow oven for about 1¼ hours or until firm. Stand for 5 minutes before turning onto wire rack to cool.

Cut cold cake into 3 layers, brush each layer with liqueur. Sandwich layers with half the cinnamon cream. Cover and decorate cake with remaining cream. Decorate with pecans and lightly sprinkle with extra cinnamon, if desired.

Cinnamon Cream: Beat cream, cinnamon and sifted icing sugar in small bowl until firm peaks form.

ABOVE: Chocolate Mallow Roll with Raspberry Sauce.
RIGHT: From top: Pecan Pumpkin Cake with Cinnamon Cream, Coconut Roulade with Cherry Cream.

Above & right: Plates from Shop 3, Balmain

CHOCOLATE MALLOW ROLL WITH RASPBERRY SAUCE

Roll can be made a day ahead; keep, covered, in refrigerator. This recipe is not suitable to freeze or microwave.

3 eggs, separated
½ cup castor sugar
¾ cup self-raising flour
2 tablespoons hot milk
MARSHMALLOW FILLING
2 teaspoons gelatine
½ cup water
½ cup castor sugar
1 teaspoon grated orange rind
2 teaspoons orange juice
CHOCOLATE GLAZE
60g butter, melted
200g dark chocolate, melted
¼ cup light corn syrup
RASPBERRY SAUCE
250g punnet raspberries
¼ cup icing sugar
2 tablespoons water

Lightly grease a 25cm x 30cm Swiss roll pan, cover base with paper, extending over 2 opposite sides, grease paper.

Beat eggs in small bowl with electric mixer until thick and creamy, gradually add sugar, beat until dissolved between additions. Transfer mixture to large bowl. Fold in sifted flour and milk in 2 batches. Pour into prepared pan. Bake in moderate oven for about 12 minutes or until firm. Turn roll onto sheet of paper. Remove lining paper, trim edges, roll gently from narrow end, using paper to lift cake and guide roll. Stand 5 minutes, unroll, cool to room temperature.

Spread marshmallow filling over cake, roll again. Refrigerate for 1 hour. Place roll on wire rack over tray. Pour chocolate glaze over roll. Stand at room temperature until glaze is set. Serve sliced roll with raspberry sauce.

Marshmallow Filling: Combine gelatine, water and sugar in large saucepan, stir over heat, without boiling, until sugar and gelatine are dissolved. Bring to boil, uncovered, without stirring, for 6 minutes. Remove from heat, cool to room temperature. Pour mixture into small bowl, add rind and juice, beat with electric mixer until thick; use immediately.

Chocolate Glaze: Combine butter, chocolate and corn syrup in medium bowl; stand 5 minutes before using.

Raspberry Sauce: Blend or process berries, sugar and water until smooth; strain before using.

LIME COCONUT BAKE

Desserts can be made a day ahead; keep, covered, in refrigerator. This recipe is not suitable to freeze or microwave.

1 tablespoon chopped glacé ginger
2 tablespoons chopped roasted unsalted macadamias
4 eggs, lightly beaten
400ml can coconut cream
2 teaspoons grated lime rind
¼ teaspoon ground ginger
½ teaspoon ground cinnamon
½ cup brown sugar
¼ cup golden syrup
¼ cup lime juice

Lightly grease 6 ovenproof moulds (¾ cup capacity).

Sprinkle base of moulds with combined glacé ginger and nuts. Combine eggs and coconut cream in medium bowl, stir in rind, ground ginger and cinnamon. Place sugar, golden syrup and juice in small saucepan, stir over heat, without boiling, until sugar is dissolved, cool to room temperature. Stir into egg mixture, pour into prepared moulds.

Place moulds in baking dish, then pour in enough boiling water to come halfway up sides of moulds, bake in moderate oven for about 1 hour or until just set. Remove moulds from water; cool, refrigerate overnight.

Turn desserts onto plates, serve with whipped cream and toasted shredded coconut, if desired.

Serves 6.

PASSIONFRUIT CREAMS

You will need about 5 passionfruit for this recipe. Desserts can be made a day ahead; keep, covered, in refrigerator. This recipe is not suitable to freeze or microwave.

300ml carton thickened cream
⅓ cup passionfruit pulp
4 egg yolks
¼ cup castor sugar

Bring cream to boil in medium saucepan, add passionfruit, reduce heat, simmer, uncovered, for 3 minutes. Remove from heat, stand 15 minutes, strain to remove seeds.

Beat egg yolks and sugar in small bowl with electric mixer until thick and creamy, gradually beat in warm cream mixture.

Place 4 ovenproof dishes (⅓ cup capacity) into baking dish, pour custard into dishes, cover with foil or lids. Pour enough boiling water into baking dish to come halfway up sides of dishes. Bake in slow oven for about 35 minutes or until mixture is just set; cool, refrigerate overnight. Serve with extra cream, if desired.

Serves 4.

ABOVE: Lime Coconut Bake.
RIGHT: Passionfruit Creams.

Right: Plate from Paraphernalia; cloth from Casa Shopping

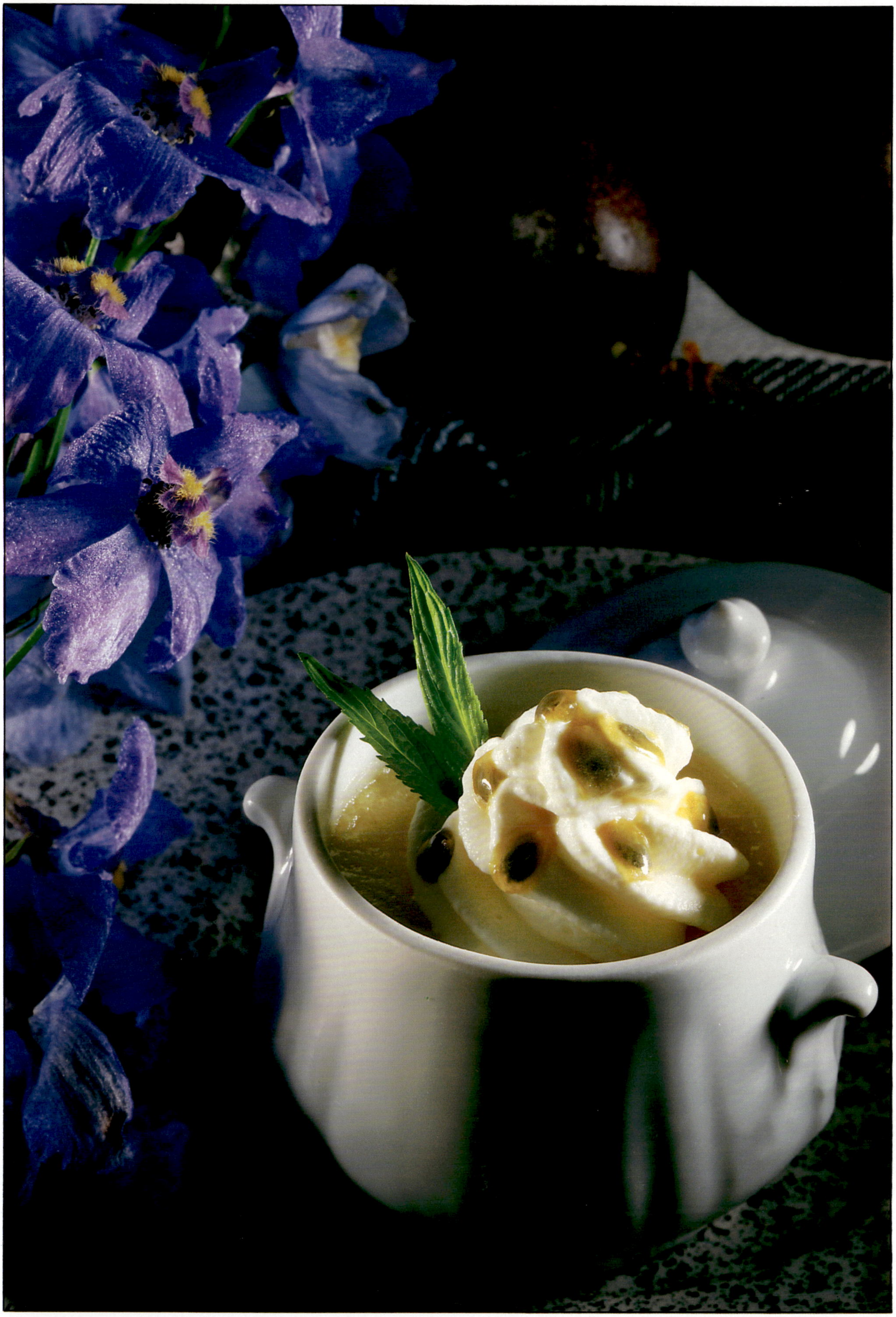

NOUGAT ALMOND CUSTARD

We used Callard & Bowser dessert nougat for this recipe. Amaretto is an almond-flavoured liqueur. Recipe can be made a day ahead; keep, covered, in refrigerator. This recipe is not suitable to freeze or microwave.

30g butter
70g packet dessert nougat
½ cup castor sugar
¼ cup water
1 egg
3 egg yolks
1½ tablespoons Amaretto
1 teaspoon gelatine
1 tablespoon water, extra
300ml carton thickened cream

Melt butter in medium saucepan, add nougat, stir over heat, without boiling, until nougat is melted. Stir in sugar and water, stir over heat, without boiling, until sugar is dissolved. Bring to boil, boil, uncovered, without stirring, for about 3 minutes or until syrup is slightly thickened.

Beat egg and egg yolks in small bowl with electric mixer until thick and creamy, beat in liqueur. Gradually beat in hot nougat syrup while motor is operating.

Sprinkle gelatine over extra water in small bowl, stand in small pan of simmering water (or microwave on HIGH for about 15 seconds), stir until dissolved, cool slightly. Gradually beat gelatine mixture into nougat mixture.

Transfer mixture to large bowl. Beat cream in small bowl until soft peaks form, fold into nougat mixture. Pour mixture into 6 glasses (½ cup capacity). Decorate with toffee pieces, if desired.

Serves 6.

BELOW: From top: Nougat Almond Custard, Brandied Apricot Trifle.
RIGHT: Ginger Crème Caramels.

Below: Glass, bowl and plate from Dansab; basket from The Australian East India Co. Right: Plate from Studio-Haus.

BRANDIED APRICOT TRIFLE

Jam rollettes are mini Swiss rolls. Trifle is best prepared a day ahead; keep, covered, in refrigerator. This recipe is not suitable to freeze or microwave.

**2 cups milk
1 tablespoon custard powder
¼ cup brown sugar
4 eggs
1 teaspoon vanilla essence
825g can apricots
750ml can apricot nectar
2 tablespoons gelatine
250g packet jam rollettes
⅓ cup brandy
300ml carton thickened cream**

Bring milk to boil in medium saucepan, remove from heat. Blend custard powder and sugar with eggs in medium bowl. Beat with electric mixer until sugar is dissolved. Stir egg mixture into milk, stir over heat, without boiling, until custard is slightly thickened; stir in essence, cover, cool to room temperature.

Drain apricots, reserve syrup. Combine reserved syrup and apricot nectar in medium saucepan, sprinkle with gelatine, stir over heat, without boiling, until gelatine is dissolved; cool to room temperature. Slice apricots, place into 19cm x 29cm lamington pan. Pour gelatine mixture over apricots; refrigerate until set. Cut rollettes into 1cm slices, arrange half the slices over base of serving dish (12 cup capacity). Sprinkle cake with half the brandy. Cut apricot jelly into 5cm pieces, arrange half the jelly over cake, top with half the custard. Repeat layering with cake, brandy, jelly and custard. Beat cream in small bowl until soft peaks form, spread over trifle. Decorate trifle with extra apricots, if desired.

Serves 8.

GINGER CREME CARAMELS

Dessert is best prepared a day ahead; keep, covered, in refrigerator. Recipe unsuitable to freeze or microwave.

**¾ cup castor sugar
¾ cup water
2 tablespoons finely chopped glacé ginger
4 eggs
1 teaspoon vanilla essence
¼ cup castor sugar, extra
1¼ cups milk
¾ cup thickened cream**

Combine sugar, water and ginger in medium saucepan, stir over heat, without boiling, until sugar is dissolved. Bring to boil, boil, uncovered, without stirring, for 2 minutes; strain sugar syrup. Return sugar syrup to same pan, return to boil, boil, uncovered, without stirring, for about 3 minutes or until golden brown.

Pour caramel mixture into 6 ovenproof dishes (¾ cup capacity).

Whisk eggs, essence and extra sugar together in medium bowl. Combine milk and cream in medium saucepan, bring to boil, remove from heat, allow bubbles to subside; gradually whisk into egg mixture. Strain prepared custard into jug. Place prepared dishes into baking dish, pour custard into dishes. Pour enough boiling water into baking dish to come half-way up sides of dishes. Bake in moderate oven for about 25 minutes or until custard is just set. Remove dishes from water, cool to room temperature; refrigerate overnight.

Turn custards onto plates, serve with extra glacé ginger and strawberries, if desired.

Serves 6.

CREAMY LEMON CRUMBLE

Dessert can be prepared several hours ahead; keep, covered, in refrigerator. This recipe is not suitable to freeze or microwave.

1 tablespoon cornflour
½ cup castor sugar
2 teaspoons grated lemon rind
½ cup lemon juice
2 tablespoons water
3 eggs, lightly beaten
15g butter
⅓ cup sour cream
CRUMBLE TOPPING
½ cup plain flour
1 cup minute oats
125g butter
2 tablespoons castor sugar
¼ cup shredded coconut
½ cup slivered almonds
¼ cup currants

Grease 4 ovenproof dishes (1 cup capacity). Blend cornflour and sugar with rind, juice and water in top of double saucepan (or heatproof bowl), stir in eggs and butter. Stir over simmering water until mixture is thickened. Remove from heat, stir in sour cream.

Pour custard into prepared dishes, sprinkle with topping. Bake in moderately hot oven for about 20 minutes or until topping is crisp.

Crumble Topping: Sift flour into medium bowl, stir in oats, rub in butter. Stir in remaining ingredients.

Serves 4.

FRIED ALMOND CUSTARD WITH PLUM SAUCE

Amaretto is an almond-flavoured liqueur. Custard and sauce can be prepared 2 days ahead; keep, covered, in refrigerator. This recipe is not suitable to freeze.

300ml carton thickened cream
2½ cups milk
½ cup custard powder
2 tablespoons plain flour
⅔ cup castor sugar
1 tablespoon Amaretto
extra plain flour
1 egg, lightly beaten
1 tablespoon milk, extra
½ cup packaged ground almonds
½ cup packaged breadcrumbs
oil for deep-frying
PLUM SAUCE
425g can dark plums
1 cinnamon stick
¼ teaspoon grated lemon rind
1 teaspoon cornflour
¼ cup water
3 teaspoons Amaretto

Line base and sides of 23cm square slab pan with foil.

Combine cream and 1½ cups of the milk in medium saucepan, bring to boil, remove from heat. Blend custard powder, flour and sugar with remaining milk in medium bowl, stir into hot milk mixture. Stir over high heat until mixture boils and thickens, stir in liqueur, pour into prepared pan. Cool to room temperature, cover; refrigerate until firm.

Cut custard into 12 pieces about 5cm x 7cm. Toss custard pieces in extra flour, shake away excess flour. Dip pieces into combined egg and extra milk, toss in combined almonds and breadcrumbs, pressing mixture on firmly. Refrigerate for 15 minutes. Deep-fry custard pieces in hot oil until golden brown; drain on absorbent paper; serve with sauce.

Plum Sauce: Drain plums, reserve ⅓ cup of the syrup. Remove seeds from plums, blend or process plums until smooth. Combine plum purée, reserved syrup, cinnamon and rind in medium saucepan. Blend cornflour with water in small bowl, stir into pan, stir over high heat until mixture boils and thickens; remove cinnamon, stir in liqueur.

Serves 6.

COFFEE CREME CARAMELS

Tia Maria is a coffee-flavoured liqueur. Desserts are best made a day ahead; keep, covered, in refrigerator. Recipe unsuitable to freeze or microwave.

¾ cup castor sugar
¾ cup water
6 eggs
⅓ cup castor sugar, extra
2 tablespoons Tia Maria
1 tablespoon dry instant coffee
1 tablespoon water, extra
1½ cups milk
300ml carton thickened cream

Combine sugar and water in medium saucepan, stir over heat, without boiling, until sugar is dissolved. Bring to boil, boil, uncovered, without stirring, for about 5 minutes or until mixture is golden brown. Pour caramel evenly into 6 ovenproof dishes (1 cup capacity).

Whisk eggs and extra sugar together in medium bowl, stir in liqueur and combined coffee and extra water. Combine milk and cream in medium saucepan, bring to boil, remove from heat, allow bubbles to subside. Gradually whisk into egg mixture, strain into jug. Place dishes in baking dish, pour custard into dishes. Pour enough boiling water into baking dish to come halfway up sides of dishes.

Bake in moderate oven for 30 minutes or until custards are just set. Remove dishes from water; cool to room temperature, refrigerate custards

overnight. Turn custards onto serving plates, serve with extra whipped cream and orange rind, if desired.
  Serves 6.

ABOVE: Clockwise from top left: Coffee Crème Caramels, Creamy Lemon Crumble, Fried Almond Custard with Plum Sauce.

Above: Plates from The Bay Tree; caneware from The Australian East India Co

BANANA COCONUT PANCAKES

Pancakes are best prepared just before serving. Unfilled pancakes can be frozen, layered with paper, for 2 months. Filling and topping can be made 2 days ahead; keep, covered, in refrigerator. This recipe is not suitable to microwave.

BELOW: From top: Banana Coconut Pancakes, Black Forest Crêpes.
RIGHT: Buttermilk Pancakes with Spicy Apple.

Right: Plate from Shop 3, Balmain; napkin from Accoutrement

PANCAKES
1¼ cups self-raising flour
1½ tablespoons castor sugar
1 egg
1½ cups milk

BANANA COCONUT FILLING
2 tablespoons shredded coconut
90g butter
¾ cup brown sugar, firmly packed
¾ cup cream
½ cup sour cream
4 medium bananas, sliced

TOPPING
⅓ cup sour cream
2 tablespoons cream
2 teaspoons icing sugar
2 teaspoons underproof dark rum

Pancakes: Sift flour and sugar into medium bowl, make well in centre, gradually stir in combined egg and milk. Mix to a smooth batter (or blend or process all ingredients until smooth). Cover, stand for 30 minutes.

Pour 2 to 3 tablespoons of batter into heated greased heavy-based frying pan; cook until lightly browned underneath. Turn pancake, brown on other side. Repeat with remaining batter. You will need 6 pancakes for this recipe. Divide filling between pancakes, fold pancakes over, serve with topping.

Banana Coconut Filling: Toast coconut on oven tray in moderate oven for about 5 minutes or until golden brown; cool. Melt butter in medium frying pan, add brown sugar, stir over medium heat for about 1 minute (or microwave on HIGH for about 1 minute) or until sugar is dissolved. Stir in creams. Add bananas and coconut, stir gently.
Topping: Combine all ingredients in small bowl; mix well.
Serves 6.

BLACK FOREST CREPES

Kirsch is a cherry-flavoured liqueur. Assemble crêpes just before serving. Unfilled crêpes can be made 2 days ahead; keep, layered with paper, in refrigerator, or crêpes can be frozen for 2 months. This recipe is not suitable to microwave.

CREPES
¾ cup plain flour
3 eggs
1 tablespoon oil
1 cup milk
CHERRY FILLING
2 x 410g cans pitted black cherries
⅓ cup sugar
1 cinnamon stick
2 tablespoons Kirsch
1 tablespoon arrowroot
2 tablespoons water
CHOCOLATE SAUCE
100g dark chocolate, melted
½ cup cream

Crêpes: Sift flour into medium bowl, make well in centre, gradually stir in combined eggs, oil and milk. Mix to a smooth batter (or blend or process all ingredients until smooth). Cover, stand for 30 minutes.

Pour 2 to 3 tablespoons of batter into heated greased heavy-based frying pan; cook until lightly browned underneath. Turn crêpe, brown on other side. Repeat with remaining batter. You will need 8 crêpes for this recipe. Divide filling between crêpes, fold crêpes into triangles. Serve with sauce and ice cream, if desired.
Cherry Filling: Drain cherries, reserve ⅔ cup of syrup. Combine reserved syrup, sugar and cinnamon in medium saucepan, stir over heat, without boiling, until sugar is dissolved. Bring to boil, reduce heat, simmer, uncovered, without stirring, for 2 minutes; strain. Stir in cherries and liqueur. Blend arrowroot with water in small bowl, stir into cherry mixture, stir over high heat until mixture boils and thickens slightly.
Chocolate Sauce: Combine chocolate and cream in small bowl; mix well.
Serves 4.

BUTTERMILK PANCAKES WITH SPICY APPLE

Pancakes are best made close to serving time; they can be frozen, layered with paper, for 2 months. Spicy apple can be made a day ahead; keep, covered, in refrigerator. This recipe is not suitable to microwave.

BUTTERMILK PANCAKES
1 cup self-raising flour
3 eggs
1 tablespoon castor sugar
1 cup buttermilk
15g butter, melted
SPICY APPLE
4 large apples, thinly sliced
¼ cup honey
½ cup water
2 tablespoons sultanas
½ teaspoon ground cinnamon

Buttermilk Pancakes: Sift flour into large bowl. Beat eggs and sugar in small bowl with electric mixer until thick and creamy, stir in buttermilk and butter. Gradually whisk mixture into flour, whisk until smooth.

Pour 2 tablespoons batter into heated greased heavy-based frying pan. Cook over medium heat until browned underneath. Turn pancake, brown on other side. Repeat with remaining batter. You will need 12 pancakes for this recipe. Serve pancakes topped with hot spicy apple and whipped cream, if desired.
Spicy Apple: Combine apples, honey and water in medium saucepan, bring to boil, reduce heat, cover, simmer for about 10 minutes (or microwave, covered, on HIGH for about 10 minutes) or until apples are tender; stir in sultanas and cinnamon.
Serves 6.

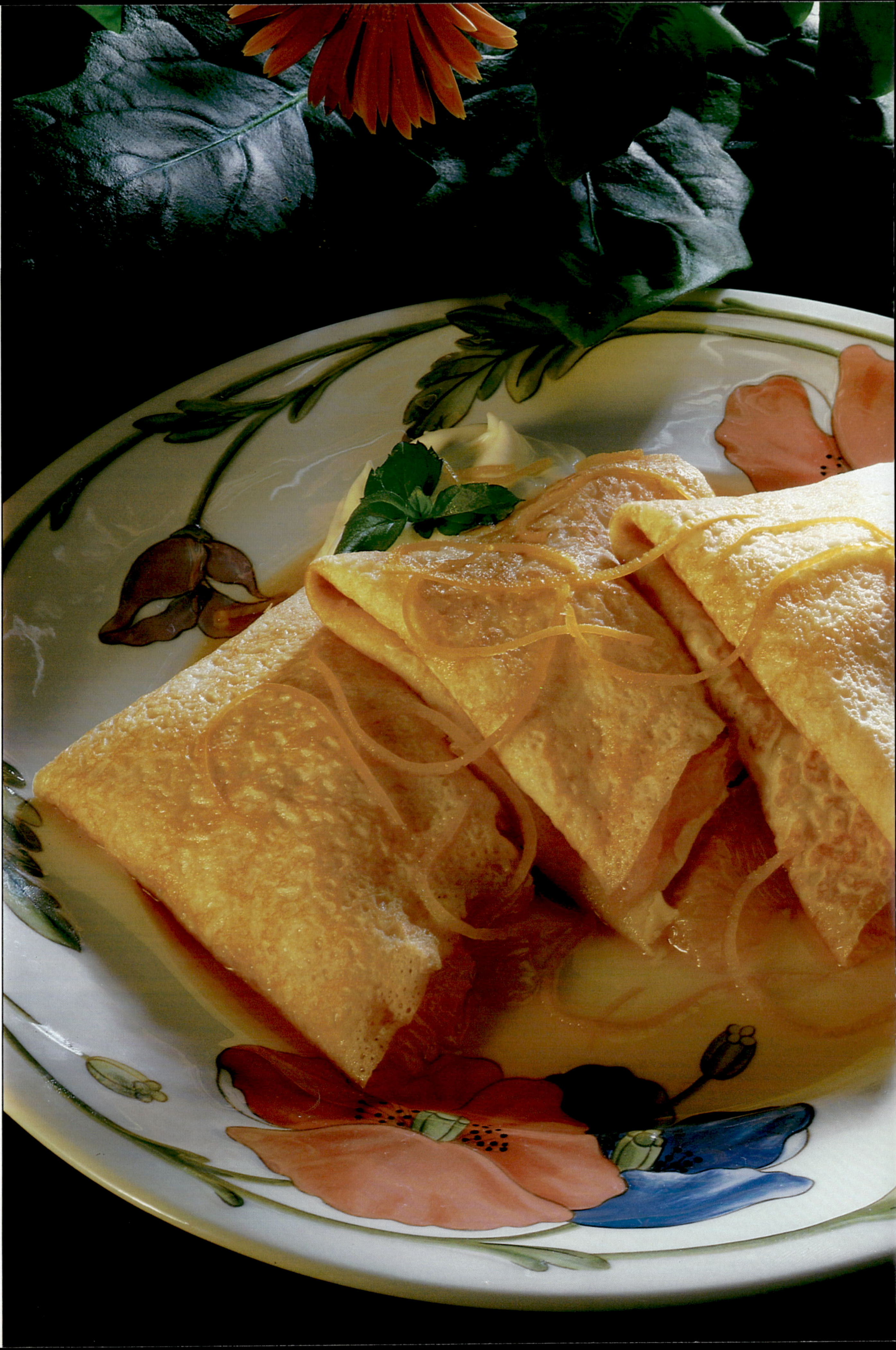

MANDARIN CREPES WITH MANDARIN SYRUP

Grand Marnier is an orange-flavoured liqueur. You will need about 6 medium mandarins for this recipe. Syrup can be made a week ahead; keep, covered, in refrigerator. Crêpes can be made 2 days ahead; keep, layered with paper, in refrigerator. Unfilled crêpes can be frozen for 2 months. This recipe is not suitable to microwave.

CREPES
¾ cup plain flour
3 eggs, lightly beaten
1 tablespoon walnut oil
1 cup milk
1 teaspoon grated mandarin rind
MANDARIN SYRUP
1 tablespoon water
½ cup castor sugar
¾ cup mandarin juice
1 tablespoon Grand Marnier
½ cup fresh or canned mandarin segments

Crêpes: Sift flour into medium bowl, make well in centre, gradually stir in combined eggs, oil, milk and rind. Mix to a smooth batter (or blend or process all ingredients until smooth). Cover, stand for 30 minutes.

Pour 2 to 3 tablespoons of batter into heated greased heavy-based frying pan; cook until lightly browned underneath. Turn crêpe, brown on other side. Repeat with remaining batter. You will need 12 crêpes for this recipe. Divide mandarin segments between crêpes, fold crêpes into triangles, serve with remaining syrup and cream, if desired.

Mandarin Syrup: Combine water and sugar in medium saucepan, stir over heat, without boiling, until sugar is dissolved. Bring to boil, boil, uncovered, without stirring, until syrup turns light golden brown. Remove from heat, stir in juice, stir over heat until toffee is melted. Stir in liqueur and mandarin segments; stir over heat until heated through.

Serves 4.

LEFT: Mandarin Crêpes with Mandarin Syrup.

Left: Plate from Shop 3, Balmain; plant from Sherringhams

TROPICAL CREPES FLAMBE

Malibu is a coconut-flavoured rum. Crêpes can be made 2 days ahead; keep, layered with paper, in refrigerator, or crêpes can be frozen for 2 months. This recipe is not suitable to microwave.

CREPES
¾ cup plain flour
3 eggs, lightly beaten
1 tablespoon oil
1 cup milk
TROPICAL FRUIT SAUCE
125g butter
½ cup castor sugar
1 teaspoon grated lime rind
1 teaspoon grated orange rind
1¼ cups tropical fruit juice
2 tablespoons lime juice
2 medium oranges, segmented
2 medium passionfruit
2 medium bananas, sliced
½ small pineapple, thinly sliced
⅓ cup underproof dark rum
2 tablespoons Malibu

Crêpes: Sift flour into medium bowl, make well in centre, gradually stir in combined eggs, oil and milk. Mix to a smooth batter (or blend or process all ingredients until smooth). Cover, stand for 30 minutes.

Pour 2 to 3 tablespoons of batter into heated greased heavy-based frying pan; cook until lightly browned underneath. Turn crêpe, brown on other side. Repeat with remaining batter. You will need 12 crêpes for this recipe. Fold crêpes into triangles, add to pan of sauce, heat through gently. Serve crêpes topped with toasted shredded coconut, if desired.

Tropical Fruit Sauce: Melt butter in large frying pan, stir in sugar, stir over heat, without boiling, until sugar is dissolved. Stir in rinds and juices, bring to boil, boil, uncovered, stirring occasionally, until sauce is golden brown. Stir in orange segments, passionfruit pulp, bananas and pineapple, stir over low heat until fruit is just soft. Heat rum in small saucepan, ignite, pour over fruit, stand until flames subside, stir in Malibu.

Serves 6.

CHOCOLATE PANCAKES WITH MINT CREAM

Crème de Menthe is a mint-flavoured liqueur. Pancakes can be made a day ahead; keep, layered with paper, in refrigerator, or pancakes can be frozen for 2 months. Liqueur cream is best made close to serving time. This recipe is not suitable to microwave.

CHOCOLATE PANCAKES
1 cup self-raising flour
2 tablespoons cocoa
½ teaspoon bicarbonate of soda
2 tablespoons castor sugar
1⅓ cups milk
1 egg, lightly beaten
15g butter, melted
1 egg white
MINT CREAM
300ml carton thickened cream
¼ cup icing sugar
1 tablespoon Crème de Menthe
2 x 35g peppermint crisp chocolate bars, chopped

Chocolate Pancakes: Sift flour, cocoa and soda into large bowl; stir in sugar. Make well in centre, gradually stir in combined milk, egg and butter; mix well. Beat egg white in small bowl until soft peaks form, fold into batter.

Pour 2 to 3 tablespoons of batter into a heated greased heavy-based frying pan, cook over medium heat until browned underneath. Turn pancake, brown on other side. Repeat with remaining batter. You will need 8 pancakes for this recipe. Serve hot with mint cream.

Mint Cream: Beat cream in small bowl until soft peaks form. Fold in sifted icing sugar, liqueur and chocolate.

Serves 4.

APRICOT SOUFFLE CREPES

Cook filled crêpes just before serving. Unfilled crêpes can be made 2 days ahead; keep, layered with paper, in refrigerator, or crêpes can be frozen for 2 months. This recipe is not suitable to microwave.

CREPES
¾ cup plain flour
3 eggs, lightly beaten
1 cup milk
APRICOT FILLING
1 cup dried apricots
2 cups water
½ teaspoon ground coriander
1 cinnamon stick
2 eggs, separated
HONEY CREAM
300g carton sour cream
¼ cup thickened cream
1 tablespoon honey
1 tablespoon brandy

Crêpes: Sift flour into medium bowl, make well in centre, gradually stir in combined eggs and milk. Mix to a smooth batter (or blend or process all ingredients until smooth). Cover, stand for 30 minutes.

Pour 2 to 3 tablespoons of batter into heated greased heavy-based frying pan; cook until lightly browned underneath. Turn crêpe, brown on other side. Repeat with remaining batter. You will need 12 crêpes for this recipe. Divide apricot filling between crêpes, fold crêpes into triangles. Place triangles onto lightly-greased oven tray, cover loosely with foil. Bake in moderately hot oven for about 15 minutes or until crêpes are puffed. Serve with honey cream.

Apricot Filling: Combine apricots, water, coriander and cinnamon stick in medium saucepan, bring to boil, reduce heat, simmer, uncovered, for about 15 minutes or until apricots are very soft. Remove cinnamon stick. Blend or process mixture until smooth. Transfer to medium bowl; cool to room temperature. Beat egg yolks into mixture. Beat egg whites in small bowl with electric mixer, until soft peaks form, fold into mixture.

Honey Cream: Combine all ingredients in small bowl; mix well.

Serves 6.

LEFT: From top: Tropical Crêpes Flambe, Chocolate Pancakes with Mint Cream.
RIGHT: From top: Apricot Soufflé Crêpes, Orange Crêpes with Coffee Liqueur Sauce.

ORANGE CREPES WITH COFFEE LIQUEUR SAUCE

Tia Maria is a coffee-flavoured liqueur. Assemble crêpes just before serving. Unfilled crêpes can be made 2 days ahead; keep, layered with paper, in refrigerator, or crêpes can be frozen for 2 months. Sauce is best made just before serving. This recipe is not suitable to microwave.

ORANGE CREPES
1 cup plain flour
2 eggs, lightly beaten
½ cup orange juice
½ cup milk
4 medium oranges, segmented
COFFEE LIQUEUR SAUCE
180g butter
¾ cup brown sugar, firmly packed
2 tablespoons Tia Maria
2 teaspoons cornflour
2 teaspoons water

Orange Crêpes: Sift flour into medium bowl, make well in centre, gradually stir in combined eggs, juice and milk. Mix to a smooth batter (or blend or process all ingredients until smooth). Cover, stand for 30 minutes.

Pour 2 to 3 tablespoons of batter into heated greased heavy-based frying pan; cook until lightly browned underneath. Turn crêpe, brown on other side. Repeat with remaining batter. You will need 8 crêpes for this recipe. Reserve some orange segments for decoration, divide remaining segments evenly between crêpes. Fold crêpes, serve with hot coffee liqueur sauce.

Coffee Liqueur Sauce: Melt butter in a medium saucepan, stir in sugar and liqueur, stir over heat, without boiling, until sugar is dissolved. Blend cornflour with water in small bowl, stir into pan, stir over high heat until sauce boils and thickens.

Serves 4.

TANGERINE PARIS-BREST

Assemble dessert close to serving time. You will need about 3 tangerines for this recipe. The pastry rings can be made a week ahead; keep in airtight container or freeze for 2 months. This recipe is not suitable to microwave.

CHOUX PASTRY
75g butter, chopped
1 cup water
1 cup plain flour
4 eggs, lightly beaten
TANGERINE CUSTARD
4 egg yolks
½ cup castor sugar
½ cup cornflour
1 cup milk
2 teaspoons grated tangerine rind
¾ cup tangerine juice
TOFFEE
1½ cups castor sugar
¾ cup water

BELOW: Ice Cream Puffs with Tamarillo Sauce.
RIGHT: Tangerine Paris-Brest.

Below: Plate and cutlery from Studio-Haus; laminate background from Abet Laminati, napkin from Les Olivades. Right: Plate from Shop 3, Balmain.

Choux Pastry: Lightly grease oven tray, mark 6 x 8cm circles on tray.

Combine butter and water in medium saucepan, bring to boil, stirring, until butter is melted. Add sifted flour all at once; stir vigorously over medium heat until mixture leaves side of pan and forms a smooth ball. Transfer mixture to small bowl of electric mixer, add eggs gradually, beating well after each addition. Spoon mixture into piping bag fitted with plain tube, pipe pastry around edge of circles on tray.

Bake in hot oven for 10 minutes, reduce heat to moderate, bake further 15 minutes or until pastries are lightly browned and crisp. Cut pastries in half horizontally to allow steam to escape, return to moderate oven for about 10 minutes or until dry and crisp; cool on wire rack.

Fill bases of pastry circles with custard; dip tops into toffee, place onto bases. Using metal spoon, drizzle remaining toffee in thin stream backwards and forwards over lightly oiled trays; when set, break into small pieces. Decorate pastries with toffee pieces just before serving.

Tangerine Custard: Blend egg yolks, sugar and cornflour with milk in medium saucepan, stir over high heat until mixture boils and thickens, cover; cool. Stir in rind and juice.

Toffee: Combine sugar and water in medium heavy-based frying pan, stir over heat, without boiling, until sugar is dissolved. Bring to boil, boil, uncovered, without stirring, for about 10 minutes or until toffee is golden brown. Use immediately.

Serves 6.

ICE CREAM PUFFS WITH TAMARILLO SAUCE

Puffs can be filled a day ahead; keep, covered, in freezer. Sauce can be made 3 days ahead; keep, covered, in refrigerator. This recipe is not suitable to microwave.

50g butter, chopped
¾ cup water
¾ cup plain flour
3 eggs
1 litre vanilla ice cream
TAMARILLO SAUCE
4 medium tamarillos, peeled, chopped
100g strawberries, chopped
⅓ cup water
¼ cup sugar

Combine butter and water in medium saucepan, bring to boil, stirring, until butter is melted. Add sifted flour all at once, stir vigorously over medium heat with wooden spoon until mixture leaves sides of pan and forms a smooth ball.

Transfer mixture to small bowl of electric mixer, add eggs 1 at a time, beating well between additions. Spoon mixture into piping bag fitted with plain tube. Pipe mounds of pastry about 3cm in diameter onto lightly greased oven trays, about 5cm apart. Bake in hot oven for 10 minutes, reduce heat to moderate, bake further 15 minutes or until puffs are browned and crisp.

Make a small slit in the side of each puff to allow steam to escape, return to moderate oven for about 10 minutes or until dry and crisp; cool. Remove any doughy centres from puffs. Fill puffs with softened ice cream, place into freezer immediately, freeze until firm, serve with sauce.

Tamarillo Sauce: Combine tamarillos, strawberries, water and sugar in medium saucepan, stir over heat, without boiling, until sugar is dissolved. Bring to boil, reduce heat, simmer, uncovered, without stirring, for about 8 minutes or until tamarillos are soft. Remove from heat, blend or process until smooth. Push purée through sieve to remove seeds. Serve warm or cold.

Serves 6.

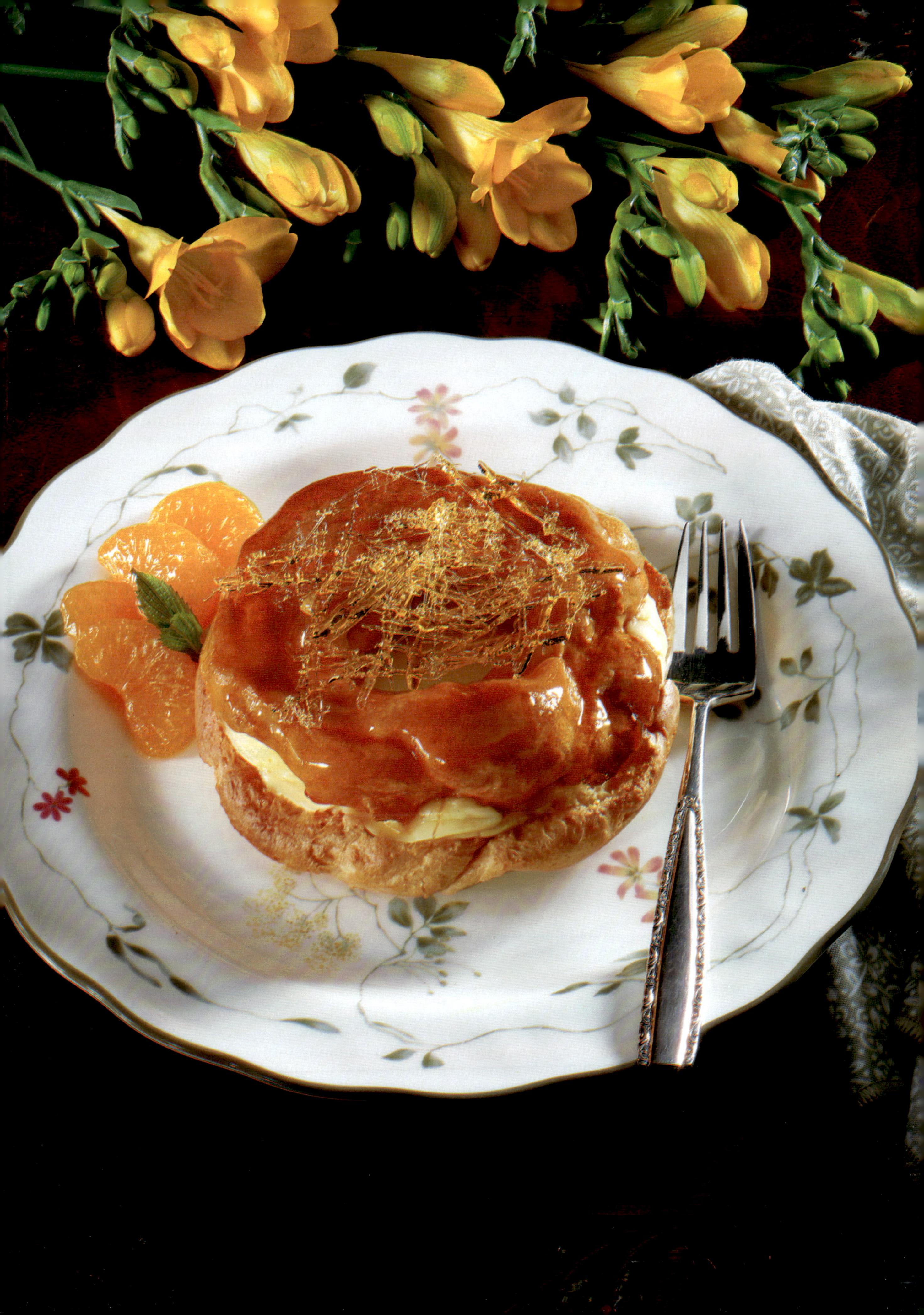

GATEAU SAINT HONORE WITH RASPBERRY CREAM

Cointreau is an orange-flavoured liqueur. Pastry base, ring and unfilled puffs can be made a day ahead; keep in airtight container or freeze for 2 months. Filling is best made on day of serving. Gâteau is best assembled close to serving time. This recipe is not suitable to microwave.

75g butter, chopped
1 cup water
1 cup plain flour
4 eggs, lightly beaten
200g punnet raspberries
¾ cup thickened cream
PASTRY BASE
1 cup plain flour
90g butter
1 egg yolk
1 tablespoon water, approximately
RASPBERRY CREAM
3 teaspoons gelatine
2 tablespoons water
200g punnet raspberries
2 x 300ml cartons thickened cream
⅓ cup icing sugar
1 tablespoon Cointreau
TOFFEE
1½ cups sugar
¾ cup water

Combine butter and water in medium saucepan, bring to boil, stirring, until butter is melted. Add sifted flour all at once, stir vigorously over medium heat with wooden spoon until mixture leaves side of pan and forms a smooth ball. Place in small bowl of electric mixer. Add eggs gradually, beating well after each addition.

Spoon one-third of mixture into piping bag fitted with plain tube, pipe 20cm ring onto lightly greased oven tray. Bake in hot oven for 10 minutes, reduce heat, bake in moderate oven further 20 minutes or until browned and well puffed. Prick all over with skewer to release steam, return to moderate oven for further 10 minutes or until dry and crisp; cool.

Place rounded teaspoons of remaining pastry about 5cm apart on lightly greased oven trays. Bake in hot oven for 10 minutes, reduce heat, bake in moderate oven further 15 minutes or until golden brown. Make a small slit in side of puffs, return to moderate oven for about 10 minutes or until dry and crisp; cool.

Roll out pastry base to 23cm round, place on oven tray, prick all over with fork, bake in hot oven for about 20 minutes or until golden brown, remove from oven, loosen; cool on tray.

Spoon one-third of raspberry cream into piping bag fitted with small plain tube, pipe raspberry cream into each puff; refrigerate for 2 hours.

Place pastry base onto plate, top with pastry ring. Fill centre of ring with

APRICOT ALMOND PITHIVIER

Dessert can be made a day ahead; keep, covered, in refrigerator. This recipe is not suitable to freeze or microwave.

375g packet frozen puff pastry, thawed
1 tablespoon apricot jam
1 egg yolk
1 teaspoon water
ALMOND PASTE LAYER
1 cup packaged ground almonds
⅓ cup castor sugar
90g unsalted butter, softened
2 egg yolks
½ teaspoon almond essence
2 tablespoons plain flour

Cut pastry in half crossways, roll out each half large enough to cut a 24cm round from each. Place 1 round onto lightly greased oven tray. Spread sieved jam evenly over pastry, leaving 2cm border; top with almond paste layer. Brush edge of pastry with combined egg yolk and water.

Top with remaining pastry round, press edges together, brush evenly with egg yolk mixture, refrigerate for 30 minutes. Brush again with egg yolk mixture; mark top and side with sharp knife to decorate. Bake in moderate oven for 35 minutes.

Almond Paste Layer: Combine all ingredients in small bowl; mix well with wooden spoon or hand. Spread mixture evenly over a piece of plastic to form a 20cm round, cover, refrigerate until firm.

remaining raspberry cream; cover, refrigerate for about 2 hours or until cream is firm.

Carefully dip bases of puffs in toffee, place on pastry ring. Spoon a little more toffee over puffs. Fill ring with raspberries and whipped cream.

Dip 2 metal spoons in toffee, press backs of spoons together, pull apart to form long threads of toffee, arrange threads decoratively on gateau.

Pastry Base: Sift flour into medium bowl, rub in butter. Add egg yolk and enough water to make ingredients cling together. Knead gently on lightly floured surface until smooth; cover, refrigerate for 30 minutes.

Raspberry Cream: Sprinkle gelatine over water in small bowl, stand in small pan of simmering water, stir until dissolved; cool to room temperature. Blend or process raspberries until smooth, sieve to remove seeds. Beat cream in large bowl until soft peaks form, fold in raspberry purée, sifted icing sugar, liqueur and gelatine mixture.

Toffee: Combine sugar and water in medium heavy-based frying pan, stir over heat, without boiling, until sugar is dissolved. Bring to boil, boil, without stirring, for about 10 minutes or until mixture is light golden brown.

PEAR AND HAZELNUT TART

Recipe can be made a day ahead; keep, covered, in refrigerator. Recipe unsuitable to freeze or microwave.

- 1½ cups plain flour
- ¼ cup packaged ground hazelnuts
- 125g butter
- 1 egg yolk
- 2 teaspoons lemon juice, approximately
- ½ cup packaged ground hazelnuts, extra
- ½ cup sultanas

FILLING
- 30g butter
- 1 medium apple, chopped
- 3 medium pears, chopped
- 2 tablespoons castor sugar
- ½ teaspoon ground cinnamon
- 1 tablespoon lemon juice
- 2 eggs, lightly beaten
- ½ cup castor sugar, extra
- ⅓ cup cream

Sift flour into medium bowl, stir in hazelnuts, rub in butter. Add egg yolk and enough juice to make ingredients cling together. Knead gently on lightly floured surface until smooth, cover, refrigerate for 30 minutes.

Roll pastry large enough to fit deep 20cm flan tin. Lift pastry into tin, trim edge. Cover pastry with paper, fill with dried beans or rice. Bake in moderately hot oven for 10 minutes, remove paper and beans, bake further 10 minutes or until lightly browned.

Sprinkle half the extra hazelnuts into pastry case, sprinkle with sultanas, top with apple mixture. Pour egg mixture over apple mixture, sprinkle with remaining hazelnuts. Bake in moderate oven for about 1 hour or until filling is firm. Serve warm or cold with extra cream, if desired.

Filling: Melt butter in medium frying pan, add apple and pears, cover, cook over medium heat for about 10 minutes or until soft, stirring occasionally. Stir in sugar, cinnamon and juice, drain. Combine eggs, extra sugar and cream in small bowl.

LEFT: From top: Apricot Almond Pithivier, Gâteau Saint Honore with Raspberry Cream.
ABOVE: Pear and Hazelnut Tart.

Above: Plate from Dansab; spoon and tea-towel from The Australian East India Co.

STRAWBERRY RHUBARB PIE

Pie can be made a day ahead; keep, covered, in refrigerator. Recipe unsuitable to freeze or microwave.

PASTRY
- 1½ cups self-raising flour
- ½ cup plain flour
- 125g butter
- 1 egg, separated
- ¼ cup water, approximately
- 1 tablespoon castor sugar

FILLING
- 4 large sticks (500g) rhubarb, chopped
- 250g punnet strawberries
- ¼ cup sugar
- ¼ cup cornflour
- ⅓ cup water

Pastry: Sift flours into large bowl, rub in butter. Make well in centre, stir in egg yolk and enough water to make ingredients cling together. Knead gently on lightly floured surface until smooth; cover, refrigerate 30 minutes.

Roll out two-thirds of the pastry large enough to line 23cm pie dish. Lift pastry into dish; trim edge. Spoon filling into dish; brush edge of pastry with egg white. Roll out remaining pastry large enough to cover filling, press edges together gently. Pinch a frill around edge.

Bake in moderately hot oven for 20 minutes, reduce heat to moderate, bake further 30 minutes or until pastry is golden brown. Brush hot pastry with egg white, sprinkle with sugar.

Filling: Combine rhubarb and strawberries in large saucepan, bring to boil, reduce heat, simmer, covered, for about 10 minutes or until rhubarb is soft; stir in sugar. Blend cornflour with water in small bowl, stir into rhubarb mixture, stir over high heat until mixture boils and thickens. Remove from heat, cool to room temperature.

GOLDEN CARROT FLAN

You will need about 2 medium carrots for this recipe. Flan can be made a day ahead; keep, covered, in refrigerator. This recipe is not suitable to freeze or microwave.

- 1 cup plain flour
- 60g butter
- 1 tablespoon castor sugar
- 2 tablespoons water, approximately
- 30g butter, extra
- 2 cups (250g) grated carrot
- ¼ cup sultanas
- 2 teaspoons plain flour, extra
- 2 teaspoons castor sugar, extra
- ¼ teaspoon ground nutmeg

FILLING
- ½ cup thickened cream
- 2 tablespoons dry white wine
- 1 egg yolk

Sift flour into medium bowl, rub in butter, stir in sugar. Stir in enough water to make ingredients cling together. Knead gently on lightly floured surface until smooth, cover, refrigerate for 30 minutes.

Roll pastry large enough to line 20cm flan tin. Lift pastry into tin, trim edge. Place tin on oven tray, cover pastry with paper, fill with dried beans or rice. Bake in moderately hot oven for 10 minutes, remove beans and paper, bake for further 10 minutes or until pastry is lightly browned.

Melt extra butter in medium frying pan, add carrot, cook over medium heat, stirring occasionally, for about 15 minutes or until carrot is tender, stir in sultanas. Combine extra flour, extra sugar and nutmeg in small bowl.

Sprinkle pastry case evenly with nutmeg mixture, top with carrot mixture; pour filling over carrot mixture. Bake in moderate oven for about 30 minutes or until filling is set. Stand for 5 minutes before serving. Dust with sifted icing sugar, if desired.
Filling: Combine cream, wine and egg yolk in small bowl.

BELOW: From top: Strawberry Rhubarb Pie, Golden Carrot Flan.
BELOW RIGHT: Tamarillo Almond Tartlets.

Below: Plate from China Doll

TAMARILLO ALMOND TARTLETS

Unfilled tartlets can be made 3 days ahead; keep in airtight container or freeze for 2 months. Fill cases just before serving. Tartlets are not suitable to microwave. Filling is not suitable to freeze.

ALMOND PASTRY
1 cup plain flour
60g butter
60g almond paste
1 egg yolk
1 tablespoon water, approximately
POACHED TAMARILLOS
6 medium tamarillos
1 cup sugar
1 cup water
¼ cup dry white wine
1 cinnamon stick
TAMARILLO CREAM
250g packet cream cheese, softened
¼ cup icing sugar
1½ teaspoons gelatine
1 tablespoon water

Almond Pastry: Lightly grease 8 x 7cm flan tins. Sift flour into large bowl, rub in butter and almond paste, make well in centre. Stir in egg yolk and enough water to make ingredients cling together. Knead gently on lightly floured surface until smooth; cover, refrigerate for 30 minutes.

Divide pastry into 8 portions, roll out each portion between sheets of paper large enough to line prepared tins. Lift pastry into tins, trim edges. Cover pastry with paper, fill with dried beans or rice. Bake in moderate oven for 10 minutes, remove paper and beans, bake further 10 minutes or until lightly browned; cool. Fill pastry cases with tamarillo cream, decorate with tamarillo slices.

Poached Tamarillos: Make small cut in base of each tamarillo, drop into saucepan of boiling water, remove from heat, stand 30 seconds, drain, peel. Combine sugar, water, wine and cinnamon in medium saucepan, stir over heat, without boiling, until sugar is dissolved, bring to boil, add tamarillos, remove from heat; cool before slicing. Transfer 3 tamarillos and sugar syrup to small bowl, refrigerate. Reserve remaining tamarillos for cream.

Tamarillo Cream: Blend or process remaining tamarillos with 1 tablespoon of the sugar syrup until smooth; strain. Beat cream cheese and sifted icing sugar in small bowl with electric mixer until fluffy, beat in tamarillo purée.

Sprinkle gelatine over water in small bowl, stand in small pan of simmering water, stir until dissolved (or microwave on HIGH for about 20 seconds); cool slightly. Beat gelatine mixture into cream cheese mixture. Refrigerate until firm.
Serves 8.

STRAWBERRY GLAZED YOGURT TARTLETS

Pastry cases can be made 3 days ahead; keep in airtight container or freeze for 2 months. Tartlets must be filled just before serving.

PASTRY
1 cup plain flour
¾ cup icing sugar
125g butter
1 egg yolk
2 teaspoons water, approximately
YOGURT FILLING
2 x 250g punnets strawberries
½ cup castor sugar
2 egg yolks
3 teaspoons gelatine
1 tablespoon port
1 tablespoon water
⅓ cup plain yogurt
½ cup thickened cream
TOPPING
1 teaspoon gelatine
¼ cup water
1 tablespoon red currant jelly

Pastry: Lightly grease 8 x 7cm flan tins. Sift flour and icing sugar into medium bowl, rub in butter. Add egg yolk and enough water to make ingredients cling together. Knead gently on lightly floured surface until smooth; cover, refrigerate for 30 minutes.

Divide pastry into 8 portions, roll portions large enough to line prepared tins. Lift pastry into tins, trim edges.

Place tins on oven tray, cover pastry with paper, fill with dried beans or rice. Bake in moderately hot oven for 10 minutes, remove paper and beans, bake for further 10 minutes or until lightly browned. Cool to room temperature.

Divide filling between pastry cases, refrigerate until set. Top filling with about half of the halved strawberries. Pour topping over strawberries, refrigerate until set.

Yogurt Filling: Blend or process remaining strawberries with sugar and egg yolks until smooth. Transfer to medium bowl. Sprinkle gelatine over port and water in small bowl, stand in small pan of simmering water, stir until dissolved (or microwave on HIGH for about 15 seconds), cool slightly. Stir gelatine mixture into strawberry mixture, fold in yogurt. Beat cream in small bowl until soft peaks form, fold into strawberry mixture.

Topping: Sprinkle gelatine over water in small bowl, stand in small pan of simmering water, stir until dissolved (or microwave on HIGH for about 30 seconds). Add jelly, stir until melted, cool; do not allow to set.

Makes 8.

BOYSENBERRY FILLO FLAN

Filling for flan can be made 2 days ahead; keep, covered, in refrigerator. Prepare flan close to serving time. This recipe is not suitable to freeze or microwave.

4 sheets fillo pastry
60g butter, melted
CAKE
125g butter
1 teaspoon vanilla essence
½ cup castor sugar
2 eggs
½ cup milk
1 cup self-raising flour
½ cup plain flour
BOYSENBERRY FILLING
2 tablespoons cornflour
1½ tablespoons water
425g can boysenberries
2 tablespoons castor sugar

Cut pastry sheets in half crossways, brush sheets with butter, layer pastry into 23cm flan tin, placing each buttered sheet at an angle so all the tin is lined with pastry.

Spread half the cake mixture into pastry case, top with filling, leaving 1cm border. Spread remaining cake mixture over filling. Place tin on oven tray. Bake in moderate oven for about 40 minutes or until golden brown. Serve dusted with sifted icing sugar.

Cake: Beat butter, essence and sugar in small bowl with electric mixer until light and fluffy; add eggs, 1 at a time, beat well between additions. Stir in milk and sifted flours in 2 batches.

Boysenberry Filling: Blend cornflour with water in medium saucepan, stir in undrained boysenberries and sugar, stir over high heat until mixture boils and thickens; cover, cool.

LEFT: From top: Boysenberry Fillo Flan, Strawberry Glazed Yogurt Tartlets.

Left: Plates from Un Jardin . . . En Plus

LEAF VOL AU VENTS WITH MANGO CREAM

You will need about 2 passionfruit for this recipe. Vol au vents can be made a day ahead; keep in airtight container. Mango cream can be made a day ahead; keep, covered, in refrigerator. Assemble dessert close to serving time. Recipe unsuitable to freeze or microwave.

375g packet frozen puff pastry, thawed
1 tablespoon milk
MANGO CREAM
1 small mango
2 egg yolks
¼ cup castor sugar
1½ tablespoons cornflour
½ cup milk
2 tablespoons passionfruit pulp

Roll out pastry on lightly floured surface to 34cm square. Cut out 18 leaf shapes 5cm x 11cm. Using a sharp knife, mark 5mm border around edge of each leaf, mark veins on leaves.

Place leaves on oven trays, brush with milk, bake in hot oven for about 7 minutes or until puffed and lightly browned; cool.

Using sharp knife, cut around borders, lift out inner sections to form lids. Fill leaves with mango cream, top with lids, dust with sifted icing sugar. Serve with extra mango and passionfruit, if desired.

Mango Cream: Blend or process mango until smooth. Beat egg yolks, sugar and cornflour in small bowl with electric mixer until thick and creamy. Heat milk in small saucepan, gradually stir in egg yolk mixture, mango and passionfruit, stir over high heat until mixture boils and thickens; cover, cool, refrigerate.

Serves 6.

PECAN GANACHE TART

Kahlua is a coffee-flavoured liqueur. Tart can be made 2 days ahead; keep, covered, in refrigerator. This recipe is not suitable to freeze or microwave.

PASTRY
½ cup pecans
1½ cups plain flour
90g butter
1 egg
1 tablespoon water, approximately

GANACHE FILLING
300ml carton thickened cream
300g dark chocolate, melted
2 tablespoons Kahlua
1 cup pecans, roughly chopped

CREAMY TOPPING
¼ cup icing sugar
300ml carton thickened cream
2 teaspoons gelatine
2 tablespoons water
1 tablespoon Kahlua

Pastry: Blend or process nuts until finely chopped (do not over-process). Sift flour into medium bowl; rub in butter, stir in nuts. Add egg and enough water to make ingredients cling together. Knead gently on lightly floured surface until smooth; cover, refrigerate for 30 minutes.

Roll pastry large enough to line 23cm flan tin. Lift pastry into flan tin; trim edge. Place tin onto oven tray, cover pastry with paper, fill with dried beans or rice. Bake in moderately hot oven for 10 minutes, remove paper and beans; bake further 10 minutes or until lightly browned. Cool to room temperature.

Spread filling into pastry case, refrigerate for about 2 hours or until filling is starting to set. Pour topping over filling, refrigerate several hours or until set. Decorate with whipped cream and extra pecans, if desired.

Ganache Filling: Combine all ingredients in a medium bowl; mix well.

Creamy Topping: Sift icing sugar into medium bowl, stir in cream. Sprinkle gelatine over water in small bowl, stand in small pan of simmering water, stir until dissolved (or microwave on HIGH for about 20 seconds); cool. Stir gelatine mixture into cream mixture, stir in liqueur.

ABOVE: Leaf Vol Au Vents with Mango Cream.
RIGHT: Pecan Ganache Tart.

Above: Plate from Mikasa. Right: Plate and cake server from China Doll.

ORANGE GLAZED CHERRY TURNOVERS

Turnovers can be prepared 2 days ahead; keep, covered, in refrigerator. Uniced turnovers can be frozen for 2 months. Turnovers are not suitable to microwave.

PASTRY
1¼ cups plain flour
¼ cup custard powder
1 tablespoon icing sugar
90g butter
¼ cup water, approximately
CHERRY FILLING
425g can pitted black cherries
1 tablespoon cornflour
1 tablespoon sugar
¼ teaspoon grated orange rind
ORANGE GLAZE
1 tablespoon orange juice
½ cup icing sugar

Pastry: Sift dry ingredients into bowl, rub in butter. Add enough water to make ingredients cling together. Knead gently on floured surface until smooth, cover, refrigerate 30 minutes.

Divide pastry into 6 portions. Roll each portion between sheets of paper into circles about 14cm in diameter. Divide cherry filling evenly over pastry rounds, moisten edges of pastry, fold over pastry to enclose filling; pinch edges together to seal.

Place turnovers on lightly greased oven tray, bake in moderately hot oven for about 20 minutes or until golden brown. Stand for 10 minutes before brushing with orange glaze.

Cherry Filling: Drain cherries, reserve one-third cup of syrup. Blend cornflour with reserved syrup in small bowl. Combine cherries, sugar and cornflour mixture in medium saucepan, stir over high heat until mixture boils and thickens; remove from heat, stir in rind; cover, cool.

Orange Glaze: Combine juice and sifted icing sugar in small bowl, stir until smooth.

Serves 6.

PASTRY APPLES WITH CINNAMON CUSTARD

Recipe is best prepared just before serving. This recipe is not suitable to freeze or microwave.

4 medium apples
1 cup water
½ cup castor sugar
¼ cup lemon juice
1 teaspoon ground cinnamon
4 sheets ready-rolled puff pastry
CINNAMON CUSTARD
¼ cup brown sugar
1 tablespoon cornflour
½ teaspoon ground cinnamon
2 cups milk
2 egg yolks
1 teaspoon vanilla essence

Peel, core and halve apples. Combine water, sugar, juice and cinnamon in medium saucepan, stir over heat, without boiling, until sugar is dissolved, bring to boil. Add apples, reduce heat, simmer, covered, for about 5 minutes or until apples are just tender; cool apples in syrup for about 30 minutes or until warm.

Cut 8 large apple shapes from pastry sheets about 12cm x 14cm. Cut 1cm strips from leftover pastry, moisten edges of pastry shapes; place strips around edges; press lightly.

Place shapes onto oven trays, bake in moderate oven for about 10 minutes or until puffed and golden brown. Drain apples, slice into fan shapes, arrange over pastry; serve with warm custard.

Cinnamon Custard: Blend sugar, cornflour and cinnamon with a little of the milk in medium saucepan, gradually stir in remaining milk. Stir over high heat until mixture boils and thickens, stir in egg yolks and essence, cover, cool before using.

Serves 8.

APPLE TARTE TATIN

It is important to use a heavy pan with an ovenproof handle. The pan we used was made from cast iron. Recipe is best prepared close to serving time. Golden Delicious apples are best when in season, but Red Delicious are an excellent substitute. This recipe is not suitable to freeze or microwave.

1 cup castor sugar
90g unsalted butter
5 medium apples, cored, quartered
PASTRY
1½ cups plain flour
125g butter, chopped
1 tablespoon castor sugar
2 tablespoons water, approximately

LEFT: from top: Orange Glazed Cherry Turnovers, Pastry Apples with Cinnamon Custard.
BELOW: Apple Tarte Tatin.

Left: Plants from Liquidambar Nursery; plates from Shop 3, Balmain

Combine sugar and butter in 23cm heavy-based frying pan, stir over heat until sugar is dissolved and mixture forms a thick golden caramel. Remove from heat.

Pack apples tightly into pan, cover with foil or lid, simmer, for 20 minutes, or until apples are tender. Remove lid, simmer uncovered, for about 1 hour or until all liquid is evaporated and caramel is dark golden brown. Remove from heat, cool for 30 minutes.

Roll pastry until large enough to cover apples in pan, lift pastry onto apples, press firmly around shape of apples. Bake in moderate oven for about 25 minutes or until pastry is golden brown and crisp. Remove from oven, stand for 5 minutes, carefully turn onto plate, serve warm.

Pastry: Sift flour into medium bowl, rub in butter, stir in sugar. Add enough water to make ingredients cling together. Knead gently on lightly floured surface until smooth; cover, refrigerate for 30 minutes.

TOFFEE PEAR FRITTERS

Fritters are best made just before serving. This recipe is not suitable to freeze or microwave.

½ cup green ginger wine
2 medium firm pears, sliced
oil for deep-frying
BATTER
½ cup plain flour
2 teaspoons castor sugar
½ teaspoon ground cinnamon
1 tablespoon oil
1 egg, separated
⅓ cup sweet white wine
TOFFEE
1 cup castor sugar
½ cup water

Pour wine over pears in small bowl, stand several hours. Drain pears on absorbent paper. Dip pears in batter, deep-fry in hot oil until golden brown; drain on absorbent paper. Place pears on serving plate, drizzle with toffee, top with toffee threads, if desired. Serve with cream or ice cream, if desired.

Batter: Sift flour, sugar and cinnamon into medium bowl, make well in centre, gradually stir in combined oil, egg yolk and wine, mix to a smooth batter. Beat egg white in small bowl until soft peaks form, fold into batter.

Toffee: Combine sugar and water in medium saucepan, stir over heat, without boiling, until sugar is dissolved. Bring to boil, boil, uncovered, without stirring, for about 10 minutes or until mixture turns golden brown.

Serves 4.

CHOCOLATE FUDGE FRITTERS

Fudge can be made several hours ahead; keep, covered, in refrigerator. Fritters are best made just before serving. This recipe is not suitable to freeze or microwave.

2 x 100g packets marshmallows, chopped
60g butter
1 tablespoon water
1 teaspoon vanilla essence
125g dark chocolate, chopped
oil for deep-frying
BATTER
1 cup self-raising flour
30g butter, melted
⅔ cup warm milk
1 egg, separated

Cover 8cm x 26cm bar pan with strip of foil, extending over opposite sides.

Combine marshmallows, butter and water in medium saucepan, stir over heat, without boiling, or until marshmallows are melted. Remove from heat, stir in essence and chocolate, beat with wooden spoon until mixture is thick and sticky. Pour into prepared pan, cover, refrigerate until set.

Turn fudge out of pan, remove foil, cut fudge into 16 squares, dip into batter. Deep-fry fritters in hot oil, a few at a time, until golden brown; drain on absorbent paper. Serve with cream or ice cream, if desired.

Batter: Sift flour into medium bowl, make well in centre, stir in combined butter, milk and egg yolk, stir until smooth. Beat egg white in small bowl until soft peaks form, fold into batter.

Serves 4.

ABOVE: Cherry Fritters with Two Sauces.
RIGHT: From top: Toffee Pear Fritters, Chocolate Fudge Fritters.

Above: Plate from Studio-Haus. Right: Table and plates from Appley Hoare Antiques

CHERRY FRITTERS WITH TWO SAUCES

Kirsch is a cherry-flavoured liqueur. Dessert is best made just before serving. This recipe is not suitable to freeze or microwave.

300g fresh cherries
oil for deep-frying
1 tablespoon castor sugar
½ teaspoon ground cinnamon
BATTER
¼ cup plain flour
2 teaspoons icing sugar
1 egg, separated
2 tablespoons milk
CHERRY SAUCE
150g fresh cherries
1 cup water
¼ cup castor sugar
2 teaspoons cornflour
2 teaspoons water, extra

CHERRY CUSTARD
1½ tablespoons castor sugar
2 egg yolks
⅔ cup milk
1 teaspoon cornflour
1 tablespoon milk, extra
1 tablespoon Kirsch

Remove stems and stones from half the cherries. Thread each pitted cherry onto a skewer; dip into batter. Drop cherries carefully from end of skewer into hot oil. Deep-fry 6 cherries at a time, turning occasionally, until golden brown. Drain on absorbent paper. Toss fritters in combined sugar and cinnamon. Serve fritters and reserved cherries with both sauces.

Batter: Sift flour and icing sugar into medium bowl, stir in combined egg yolk and milk, mix to a smooth batter. Cover, stand for 30 minutes. Beat egg white in small bowl until soft peaks form, fold into batter.

Cherry Sauce: Remove stems and stones from cherries. Combine cherries, water and sugar in small saucepan, stir over heat, without boiling, until sugar is dissolved. Bring to boil, reduce heat, cover, simmer for about 10 minutes or until cherries are very soft. Strain mixture, discard pulp, return cherry syrup to pan. Blend cornflour with extra water, stir into cherry syrup, stir over high heat until mixture boils and thickens.

Cherry Custard: Beat sugar and egg yolk in a small bowl with electric mixer until thick and creamy. Bring milk to boil in small saucepan, gradually beat into egg yolk mixture while motor is operating; return mixture to pan. Blend cornflour with extra milk, stir into mixture, stir over high heat, until mixture boils and thickens. Remove from heat, stir in liqueur.

Serves 4.

APPLE FRITTERS WITH PRALINE BUTTER

Praline butter can be made 2 months ahead; keep, wrapped, in freezer. Fritters are best made just before serving. This recipe is not suitable to microwave.

1 tablespoon dry white wine
1 tablespoon brandy
1 tablespoon water
2 tablespoons castor sugar
¼ cup chopped dried apples
2 tablespoons chopped mixed peel
½ cup self-raising flour
⅓ cup plain flour
½ cup castor sugar, extra
¼ cup coconut
¼ cup milk
1 tablespoon water, extra
1 egg, separated
oil for deep-frying
2 teaspoons grated lemon rind
PRALINE BUTTER
¼ cup roasted unsalted macadamias
¼ cup water
¼ cup castor sugar
90g unsalted butter, softened

Combine wine, brandy, water and sugar in small saucepan, stir over heat, without boiling, until sugar is dissolved. Stir in apple and peel, stir over low heat for about 5 minutes, without boiling, until apple is plump; cool. Sift flours into medium bowl, stir in 1 tablespoon of the extra sugar and coconut. Make well in centre, stir in combined milk, extra water and egg yolk; mix to a smooth batter. Stir in apple mixture. Beat egg white in small bowl until soft peaks form, fold into batter in 2 batches. Deep-fry level tablespoons of mixture in hot oil, in batches, for about 3 minutes or until golden brown and puffed. Drain on absorbent paper; toss in combined remaining extra sugar and rind. Serve with praline butter.

Praline Butter: Lightly grease oven tray, spread nuts on tray. Combine water and sugar in small saucepan, stir over heat, without boiling, until sugar is dissolved. Bring to boil, boil for about 3 minutes or until mixture is golden brown. Pour toffee over nuts; cool. Break toffee into pieces, blend or process until finely ground. Combine butter and praline in small bowl; mix well. Spoon mixture onto piece of foil, shape into a sausage. Roll mixture in foil. Freeze until firm.

Serves 4.

ABOVE: Clockwise from top: Spicy Date Fritters with Lemon Sauce, Apple Fritters with Praline Butter, Semolina Fritters with Almond Liqueur Syrup.

Above: Plates from Accoutrement

SEMOLINA FRITTERS WITH ALMOND LIQUEUR SYRUP

Amaretto is an almond-flavoured liqueur. Dessert is best made just before serving. This recipe is not suitable to freeze or microwave.

75g butter, chopped
1 cup water
½ cup plain flour
½ cup finely ground semolina
1 tablespoon castor sugar
4 eggs, lightly beaten
½ teaspoon almond essence
oil for deep-frying
¼ cup ground almonds
ALMOND LIQUEUR SYRUP
1¼ cups water
2 cups castor sugar
1 tablespoon Amaretto

Combine butter and water in medium saucepan, bring to boil, stirring, until butter is melted. Stir in sifted flour and semolina all at once; stir vigorously over heat until mixture leaves side of pan and forms a smooth ball. Transfer mixture to small bowl of electric mixer, add sugar and eggs gradually, beating well after each addition. Stir in essence. Deep-fry heaped teaspoons of mixture in hot oil, in batches, until puffed and golden brown. Drain on absorbent paper, dip in syrup, serve sprinkled with almonds.

Almond Liqueur Syrup: Combine water and sugar in medium saucepan, stir over heat, without boiling, until sugar is dissolved. Bring to boil, reduce heat, simmer, uncovered, without stirring, for 8 minutes. Remove from heat, stir in liqueur.

Serves 8.

SPICY DATE FRITTERS WITH LEMON SAUCE

Dessert is best cooked just before serving. This recipe is not suitable to freeze or microwave.

⅓ cup dried apricots
250g fresh dates
⅓ cup self-raising flour
⅓ cup cornflour
¼ teaspoon ground cinnamon
¾ cup milk
oil for deep-frying
icing sugar
LEMON SAUCE
½ cup castor sugar
1 tablespoon cornflour
1 cup water
1 tablespoon lemon butter
15g butter
1 teaspoon grated lemon rind
2 tablespoons lemon juice

Cut apricots into thin strips, place into small bowl, cover with boiling water, stand for 15 minutes; drain. Carefully remove and discard stones from dates.

Fill hollow in centre of dates with apricot strips. Sift flours and cinnamon into medium bowl, make well in centre, gradually stir in milk, mix to a smooth batter. Place dates into batter; stir until dates are well coated. Deep-fry dates in hot oil, a few at a time, until golden brown; drain on absorbent paper. Dust fritters lightly with sifted icing sugar, serve with lemon sauce and ice cream or cream, if desired.

Lemon Sauce: Combine sugar and cornflour in medium saucepan, gradually stir in water, stir until smooth. Stir in lemon butter, butter, rind and juice, stir over high heat until sauce boils and thickens.

Serves 4.

FRESH APPLE SOUFFLES

Soufflés must be made just before serving. This recipe is not suitable to freeze or microwave.

**1 medium apple, grated
2 tablespoons water
1 teaspoon grated lemon rind
1 tablespoon apricot jam
2 tablespoons castor sugar
45g butter
1 tablespoon plain flour
1 tablespoon cornflour
¾ cup milk
¼ cup apple juice
3 eggs, separated**

Combine apple, water, rind, jam and sugar in small saucepan, stir over heat, without boiling, until sugar is dissolved. Bring to boil, reduce heat, simmer, uncovered, without stirring, for about 5 minutes or until apple is tender and liquid evaporated; cool. Melt butter in medium saucepan, stir in flours, stir over medium heat for 1 minute. Remove from heat, gradually stir in milk and juice, stir over high heat until mixture boils and thickens.

Transfer mixture to large bowl, stir in apple mixture and egg yolks. Beat egg whites in small bowl with electric mixer until soft peaks form, fold into warm apple mixture in 2 batches. Place 6 ovenproof dishes (½ cup capacity) onto oven tray, spoon mixture into dishes. Bake in moderately hot oven for about 20 minutes or until puffed and lightly browned.

Serves 6.

COFFEE SOUFFLES WITH PECAN PRALINE CREAM

Soufflés must be made just before serving. This recipe is not suitable to freeze or microwave.

**30g butter
1 tablespoon plain flour
¾ cup milk
2 teaspoons dry instant coffee
2 egg yolks
¼ cup castor sugar
3 egg whites**
PECAN PRALINE CREAM
**¼ cup pecans
1½ tablespoons water
1½ tablespoons castor sugar
⅔ cup thickened cream**

Melt butter in medium saucepan, stir in flour, stir over medium heat for 1 minute. Remove from heat, gradually stir in combined milk and coffee, stir over high heat until mixture boils and thickens. Beat egg yolks and sugar in small bowl with electric mixer until thick and creamy, gradually beat in coffee mixture. Transfer mixture to large bowl. Beat egg whites in small bowl with electric mixer until soft peaks form, fold into coffee mixture in 2 batches. Pour mixture into 6 ovenproof dishes (½ cup capacity), stand on oven tray. Bake in moderately hot oven for about 15 minutes or until puffed and golden brown. Serve with pecan praline cream.

Pecan Praline Cream: Place nuts on lightly oiled tray. Combine water and sugar in small saucepan, stir over heat, without boiling, until sugar is dissolved. Bring to boil, boil, uncovered, without stirring, for about 3 minutes or until mixture turns golden brown, quickly pour over pecans; cool. Break toffee into pieces, blend or process until finely ground. Combine praline and cream in small bowl.

Serves 6.

TAMARILLO HONEY SOUFFLES

Soufflés must be made just before serving. This recipe is not suitable to freeze or microwave.

2 medium tamarillos
¼ cup water
¼ cup castor sugar
¼ cup honey
4 egg whites

Place tamarillos in a saucepan of hot water, stand for 5 minutes. Peel away skin with a sharp knife, chop tamarillos.

Combine tamarillos and water in small saucepan, bring to boil, reduce heat, simmer, uncovered, for about 5 minutes or until tamarillos are soft and pulpy. Stir in sugar and honey, stir over heat, without boiling, until sugar is dissolved. Bring to boil, boil, uncovered, without stirring, for about 10 minutes or until mixture is thick and syrupy. Beat egg whites in small bowl with electric mixer until soft peaks form. Gradually pour hot tamarillo mixture into egg whites while motor is operating. Spoon mixture into 4 ovenproof dishes (1 cup capacity), place on oven tray. Bake in moderate oven for about 15 minutes or until puffed and golden brown. Dust with sifted icing sugar, if desired.

Serves 4.

ABOVE LEFT: From top: Coffee Soufflés with Pecan Praline Cream, Fresh Apple Soufflés.
ABOVE: Tamarillo Honey Soufflés.

Above left: Plate from Dansab, jug from The Australian East India Company. Above: Plates and napkin from Oldentimes Antiques; jug from The Country Trader

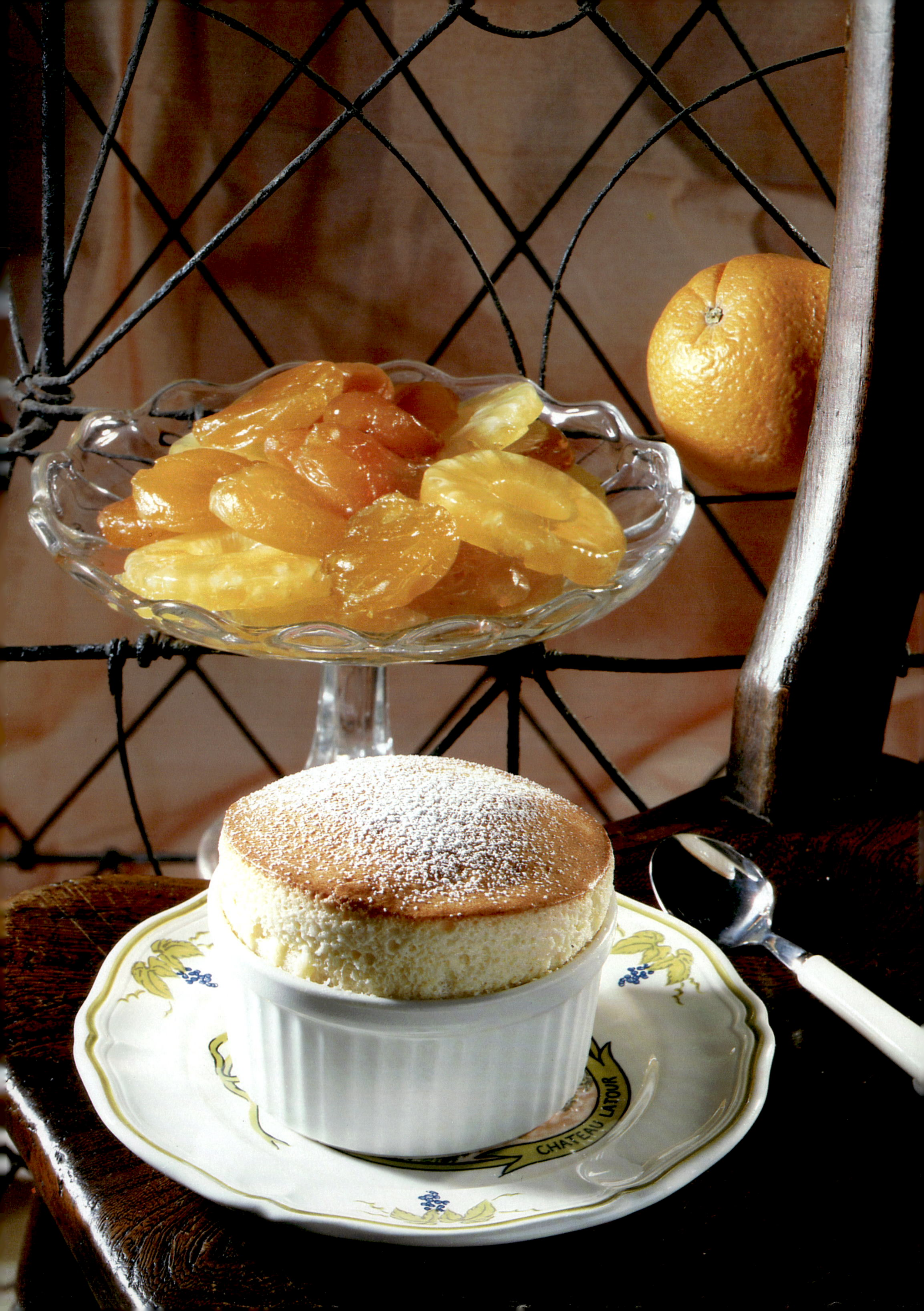
CHATEAU LATOUR

GINGER SOUFFLES

Soufflés must be made just before serving. This recipe is not suitable to freeze or microwave.

3 eggs, separated
¼ cup castor sugar
2 tablespoons plain flour
2 teaspoons ground ginger
¾ cup boiling milk

Combine egg yolks and sugar in small bowl, beat with electric mixer until thick and creamy. Beat in sifted flour and ginger. Transfer mixture to top of double saucepan (or heatproof bowl). Gradually whisk in milk, whisk over simmering water until thickened slightly, transfer to large bowl. Cool for 15 minutes.

Beat egg whites in small bowl with electric mixer until soft peaks form. Fold into milk mixture in 2 batches. Pour into 6 ovenproof dishes (¾ cup capacity); stand on oven tray. Bake in moderately hot oven for about 15 minutes or until puffed and golden brown. Dust with sifted icing sugar before serving, if desired.

Serves 6.

ORANGE LIQUEUR SOUFFLES WITH MACERATED FRUITS

Grand Marnier is an orange-flavoured liqueur. Soufflés must be made just before serving. This recipe is not suitable to freeze or microwave.

3 glacé apricots, chopped
3 rings glacé pineapple, chopped
2 tablespoons Grand Marnier
60g butter
2 tablespoons plain flour
2 teaspoons grated orange rind
¼ cup castor sugar
2 tablespoons Grand Marnier, extra
½ cup milk
¼ cup thickened cream
5 eggs, separated

Grease 6 ovenproof dishes (1 cup capacity), sprinkle with a little extra castor sugar. Combine glacé fruit and liqueur in small bowl; cover, stand for 30 minutes. Place fruit mixture into prepared dishes.

Melt butter in medium saucepan, stir in flour, stir over medium heat for 1 minute. Remove from heat, gradually stir in combined rind, sugar, extra liqueur, milk and cream. Stir over high heat until mixture boils and thickens. Remove from heat, transfer to large bowl, stir in egg yolks.

Beat egg whites in medium bowl with electric mixer until soft peaks form. Fold into egg mixture in 2 batches. Pour mixture into prepared dishes, place on oven tray, bake in moderately hot oven for about 20 minutes or until puffed and golden brown. Sprinkle with sifted icing sugar, if desired.

Serves 6.

LEFT: Orange Liqueur Soufflés with Macerated Fruits.
BELOW: Ginger Soufflés.

Left: Chair and glass dish from The Country Trader; china and spoon from Studio-Haus. Below: Egg rack and whisk from The Country Trader.

TANGY LEMON SOUFFLE

Soufflé must be made just before serving. This recipe is not suitable to freeze or microwave.

**90g butter
1 tablespoon grated lemon rind
⅓ cup castor sugar
1 tablespoon plain flour
1 tablespoon cornflour
2 tablespoons lemon juice
1 cup warm milk
4 eggs, separated
2 egg whites, extra**

Cream butter, rind and sugar in small bowl until light and fluffy. Beat in sifted flours and juice; stir in milk. Transfer mixture to medium saucepan, stir over high heat until mixture boils and thickens. Transfer mixture to large bowl, stir in egg yolks.

Beat all egg whites in large bowl with electric mixer until soft peaks form, fold gently into lemon mixture in 2 batches. Pour into ovenproof dish (3 cup capacity). Bake in moderately hot oven for about 35 minutes or until puffed and golden brown. Dust with sifted icing sugar, if desired.

Serves 6.

CHOCOLATE LIQUEUR SOUFFLES

Crème de Cacao is a chocolate-flavoured liqueur. Soufflés must be made just before serving. This recipe is not suitable to freeze or microwave.

**1½ cups milk
2 tablespoons Crème de Cacao
125g dark chocolate, chopped
60g butter
¼ cup plain flour
¼ cup castor sugar
4 eggs, separated
2 egg whites, extra**

Lightly grease 4 ovenproof dishes (1 cup capacity), sprinkle with a little extra castor sugar.

Combine milk, liqueur and chocolate in medium saucepan, stir over low heat until chocolate is melted. Melt butter in separate medium saucepan, stir in flour, stir over medium heat for 1 minute. Remove from heat, gradually stir in chocolate mixture and sugar, stir over high heat until mixture boils and thickens. Transfer to large bowl, stir in egg yolks.

Beat all egg whites in large bowl with electric mixer until soft peaks form. Fold egg whites into chocolate mixture in 2 batches. Pour into prepared dishes, stand on oven tray. Bake in moderately hot oven for about 25 minutes or until puffed and well browned. Dust with sifted icing sugar, if desired.

Serves 4.

CHOCOLATE BROWNIES WITH RASPBERRY SAUCE

Brownies are best made close to serving time. Sauce can be made a day ahead; keep, covered, in refrigerator. Recipe unsuitable to microwave.

125g butter
1 teaspoon vanilla essence
1 cup brown sugar, firmly packed
4 eggs
1 cup plain flour
¾ cup chopped unroasted hazelnuts
200g dark chocolate, melted
200g white chocolate, melted

RASPBERRY SAUCE
¾ cup raspberry jam
¼ cup water
2 teaspoons cornflour
1 tablespoon water, extra

Grease deep 20cm square cake pan, cover base with foil, grease foil.

Beat butter, essence and sugar in small bowl with electric mixer until light and fluffy. Beat in eggs 1 at a time, beating well after each addition; stir in sifted flour and nuts.

Divide mixture into 2 bowls. Stir dark chocolate into 1 bowl, spread into prepared pan. Stir white chocolate into remaining bowl, spread over dark chocolate mixture. Bake in moderate oven for about 45 minutes or until golden brown. Turn onto plate, serve hot with sauce; dust with sifted icing sugar, if desired.

Raspberry Sauce: Combine jam and water in small saucepan, stir over heat until jam is melted. Add blended cornflour and extra water, stir over high heat until sauce boils and thickens.

Serves 6.

ABOVE: Chocolate Brownies with Raspberry Sauce.
TOP LEFT: Tangy Lemon Soufflé.
LEFT: Chocolate Liqueur Soufflés.

Top Left: Soufflé dish and stand from The Bay Tree
Above: Plate and fork from Mikasa

PECAN DUMPLINGS IN HONEY SYRUP

Dumplings are best made close to serving time. This recipe is not suitable to freeze or microwave.

**1⅓ cups self-raising flour
½ teaspoon mixed spice
30g butter
½ cup chopped pecans
⅓ cup milk
1 egg, lightly beaten
HONEY SYRUP
1 cup sugar
⅓ cup honey
2½ cups water
30g butter**

Sift flour and spice into large bowl, rub in butter, stir in nuts. Make well in centre, stir in combined milk and egg. Turn dough onto lightly floured surface, knead gently until smooth. Divide dough into 12 pieces, knead each piece into a smooth ball. Place balls into simmering honey syrup, simmer, covered, for about 20 minutes or until syrup is thickened and dumplings are cooked through. Serve hot dumplings with honey syrup and ice cream, if desired.

Honey Syrup: Combine sugar, honey, water and butter in large saucepan, stir over heat, without boiling, until sugar is dissolved. Bring to boil, reduce heat to simmer before adding dumplings.

Serves 6.

RHUBARB AND APPLE COBBLER

Dessert is best made close to serving time. This recipe is not suitable to freeze or microwave.

**2 medium apples
8 sticks (600g) rhubarb, chopped
½ cup castor sugar
½ cup water
¼ teaspoon ground ginger
½ cup self-raising flour
¼ cup plain flour
2 tablespoons castor sugar, extra
60g butter
1 egg, lightly beaten
2 tablespoons milk, approximately**

Cut each apple into 8 wedges. Combine apple, rhubarb, sugar, water and ginger in medium saucepan, stir over heat, without boiling, until sugar is dissolved. Bring to boil, reduce heat, simmer, covered, for about 5 minutes or until mixture is pulpy, spread into ovenproof dish (4 cup capacity).

Sift flours into medium bowl, stir in extra sugar, rub in butter, stir in egg and enough milk to make a soft consistency. Drop heaped tablespoons of mixture around edge of fruit mixture, bake in moderate oven for about 35 minutes or until golden brown. Sprinkle with sifted icing sugar, if desired.

Serves 6.

ABOVE: From left: Pecan Dumplings in Honey Syrup, Rhubarb and Apple Cobbler.
ABOVE RIGHT: From left: Macaroon Peaches, Sweet Fried Ravioli.

Above: Plate from Appley Hoare Antiques

MACAROON PEACHES

Grand Marnier is an orange-flavoured liqueur. Peaches can be prepared ready for cooking, 3 hours ahead; keep, covered, in refrigerator. This recipe is not suitable to freeze or microwave.

4 medium slipstone peaches, halved
10 coconut macaroons, crushed
2 tablespoons chopped mixed peel
¼ teaspoon ground cinnamon
1 tablespoon Grand Marnier
⅓ cup sweet white wine
2 tablespoons castor sugar

Place peaches, cut side up, in ovenproof dish. Combine macaroons, peel, cinnamon and liqueur in small bowl. Spoon mixture into peaches, sprinkle with wine and sugar. Bake, uncovered, in moderate oven for about 25 minutes or until peaches are soft.
Serves 4.

SWEET FRIED RAVIOLI

Ravioli can be prepared several hours ahead; keep, covered with tea-towel, in refrigerator. Cook ravioli close to serving time. This recipe is not suitable to freeze or microwave.

1 cup plain flour
1 egg
1 tablespoon oil
2 teaspoons water
oil for deep-frying
RICOTTA FILLING
¼ cup sultanas
1 tablespoon underproof dark rum
125g ricotta cheese
1 teaspoon grated lemon rind
1 egg yolk, lightly beaten
2 teaspoons castor sugar
ORANGE SYRUP
½ cup castor sugar
2 teaspoons grated orange rind
½ cup orange juice
½ cup water
125g butter, chopped

Process flour, egg, oil and water until combined. Turn dough onto lightly floured surface, knead for about 5 minutes or until smooth. Roll very thin sheets of pasta using a rolling pin. (If using a pasta machine, follow manufacturer's directions.)

Using 6cm cutter, cut rounds from pasta, keep covered with a tea-towel. Place a level teaspoon of ricotta filling on each round, moisten edges with water, fold in half, pinch edges together to seal. Deep-fry ravioli in batches in hot oil until lightly browned; drain on absorbent paper. Serve warm ravioli with orange syrup.
Ricotta Filling: Combine sultanas and rum in small bowl, stand for 20 minutes, stir in remaining ingredients.
Orange Syrup: Combine sugar, rind, juice and water in small saucepan, stir over heat, without boiling, until sugar is dissolved, bring to boil, reduce heat, simmer, uncovered, for 3 minutes. Gradually whisk in butter.
Serves 6.

PLUM CLAFOUTI

Clafouti is best made just before serving. Any canned or stewed fruit can be used. This recipe is not suitable to freeze or microwave.

825g can plums, drained, pitted
½ cup self-raising flour
¼ cup castor sugar
2 eggs
½ cup milk
90g butter, melted

Place plums in greased shallow ovenproof dish (3 cup capacity).

Sift flour and sugar into medium bowl, make well in centre, gradually stir in combined eggs, milk and butter, stir until smooth. Spoon mixture evenly between plums. Bake in moderately hot oven for about 30 minutes or until firm and golden brown. Serve hot with cream, if desired.

Serves 4.

POACHED PEARS WITH ORANGE LIQUEUR SAUCE

Galliano is an aniseed-flavoured liqueur. Dessert is best made close to serving time. Sauce can be made a day ahead; keep, covered, in refrigerator. This recipe is not suitable to freeze.

⅓ cup coconut
⅓ cup packaged ground almonds
2 teaspoons grated orange rind
1 egg, separated
2 large pears
1 tablespoon apricot jam, warmed, sieved
½ cup dry white wine
½ cup water
ORANGE LIQUEUR SAUCE
90g butter
¼ cup brown sugar
1 teaspoon grated orange rind
1½ cups orange juice
¼ cup Galliano
2 teaspoons cornflour
2 teaspoons water

Combine coconut, almonds, rind and egg yolk in small bowl; mix well. Beat egg white in small bowl with electric mixer until soft peaks form, fold into coconut mixture. Peel pears, halve, remove cores, cut each half crossways into 8 slices. Spoon coconut mixture between slices.

Keeping halves together, place in shallow ovenproof dish in single layer. Spread jam over pear slices. Pour in combined wine and water, cover, bake in moderate oven for about 30 minutes (or microwave on HIGH for about 10 minutes) or until pears are tender. Remove pears from liquid, drain on absorbent paper. Serve with sauce and toasted shredded coconut, if desired.

Orange Liqueur Sauce: Melt butter in medium saucepan, add sugar, stir over heat until sugar is melted and golden brown. Stir in rind, juice and liqueur, stir over heat until toffee pieces are melted. Bring to the boil, boil until reduced by about one-third. Blend cornflour with water in small bowl, stir into pan, stir over high heat until mixture boils and thickens.

Serves 4.

COCONUT SAVARIN WITH CUMQUATS

Cumquats are best poached and soaked for 3 days before required. Malibu is a coconut-flavoured liqueur. Savarin can be made a day ahead; keep in airtight container. Savarin can be frozen for 2 months. This recipe is not suitable to microwave.

60g butter
3 teaspoons castor sugar
15g compressed yeast
¼ cup warm water
1 cup plain flour
⅓ cup coconut
2 eggs, lightly beaten
POACHED CUMQUATS
500g cumquats
1 cup sugar
2 cups water
½ cup Malibu
SYRUP
½ cup sugar
½ cup water
2 tablespoons Malibu
APRICOT GLAZE
½ cup apricot jam
2 tablespoons Malibu

Lightly grease 22cm savarin pan. Beat butter and sugar in small bowl until combined. Combine yeast and water in small bowl, stir until dissolved. Sift flour into large bowl, stir in coconut, make well in centre. Add yeast mixture, butter mixture and eggs, mix with hand until well combined. Scrape down side of bowl, cover, stand in warm place for about 30 minutes or until dough is doubled in size.

Beat again with hand until smooth and elastic. Spread mixture evenly into prepared pan, cover, stand in warm place for about 20 minutes or until dough has risen to top of pan.

Bake in hot oven for 5 minutes, reduce heat to moderate, bake further 15 minutes or until savarin feels firm. Loosen edges, turn onto wire rack, place over tray.

Drain cumquats, mix cumquat liquid with syrup, pour over hot savarin; cool. Place savarin onto plate, pour over any remaining syrup in tray, stand until all syrup has been absorbed. Brush savarin with glaze, fill with cumquats. Serve with cream, if desired.

Poached Cumquats: Pierce holes all over cumquats with skewer or toothpick. Combine sugar, water and liqueur in medium saucepan, stir over heat, without boiling, until sugar is dissolved; add cumquats. Bring to boil, reduce heat, simmer, uncovered, without stirring, for 40 minutes, remove from heat; cool cumquats in liquid.

Syrup: Combine sugar and water in small saucepan, stir over heat, without boiling, until sugar is dissolved, bring to boil, reduce heat, simmer, uncovered, without stirring, for 2 minutes. Stir in liqueur.

Apricot Glaze: Combine jam and liqueur in small saucepan, stir over heat until combined, strain; use while hot.

LEFT: Plum Clafouti.
BELOW LEFT: Poached Pears with Orange Liqueur Sauce.
BELOW: Coconut Savarin with Cumquats.

Left: Plate from The Country Trader. Below: Plate from Corso de Fiori.

TANGELO SYRUP PUDDING

Pudding is best made close to serving time. Pudding can be frozen for 2 months. This recipe is not suitable to microwave.

2 large tangelos
125g butter
½ cup castor sugar
2 eggs
1 cup wholemeal self-raising flour
½ cup white self-raising flour
½ teaspoon bicarbonate of soda
¼ cup buttermilk
SYRUP
½ cup castor sugar
60g butter

Grease pudding steamer (7 cup capacity), line base with paper, grease paper. Squeeze juice from tangelos, reserve juice for syrup; you will need ⅔ cup juice. Blend or process remaining skin and pulp until smooth.

Cream butter and sugar in small bowl with electric mixer until light and fluffy. Beat in eggs, 1 at a time, beat well between additions. Stir in sifted flours, soda and buttermilk in 2 batches. Stir in puréed tangelo pulp.

Pour mixture into prepared steamer, cover with greased round of paper, then foil; secure with string or cover with lid. Place steamer into large saucepan with enough boiling water to come halfway up side of steamer, cover, boil for 1½ hours. Stand wire rack over shallow tray, turn pudding onto rack, pour hot syrup over pudding. Serve pudding with any excess syrup and cream, if desired.

Syrup: Combine sugar, reserved juice and butter in small saucepan, stir over heat, without boiling, until sugar is dissolved. Bring to boil, reduce heat, simmer, uncovered, without stirring, for 3 minutes.

MANDARIN SYRUP DUMPLINGS

You will need about 3 medium mandarins for this recipe. Dumplings are best made close to serving time. This recipe is not suitable to freeze or microwave.

30g butter
½ cup brown sugar
½ cup golden syrup
1 cup water
¾ cup mandarin juice
DUMPLINGS
1¼ cups self-raising flour
30g butter
2 teaspoons grated mandarin rind
⅓ cup golden syrup
⅓ cup milk

Combine butter, sugar, golden syrup, water and juice in large saucepan. Stir over heat until butter is melted, bring to boil, reduce heat, add dumplings, cover, simmer for about 25 minutes or until dumplings are firm. Serve hot dumplings with syrup mixture and cream, if desired.

Dumplings: Sift flour into medium bowl, rub in butter, make well in centre. Stir in combined rind, golden syrup and milk, mix to a moist dough. Using lightly floured hands, shape level tablespoons of mixture into balls.

Serves 4 to 6.

LEFT: Mandarin Syrup Dumplings.
BELOW: Tangelo Syrup Pudding.

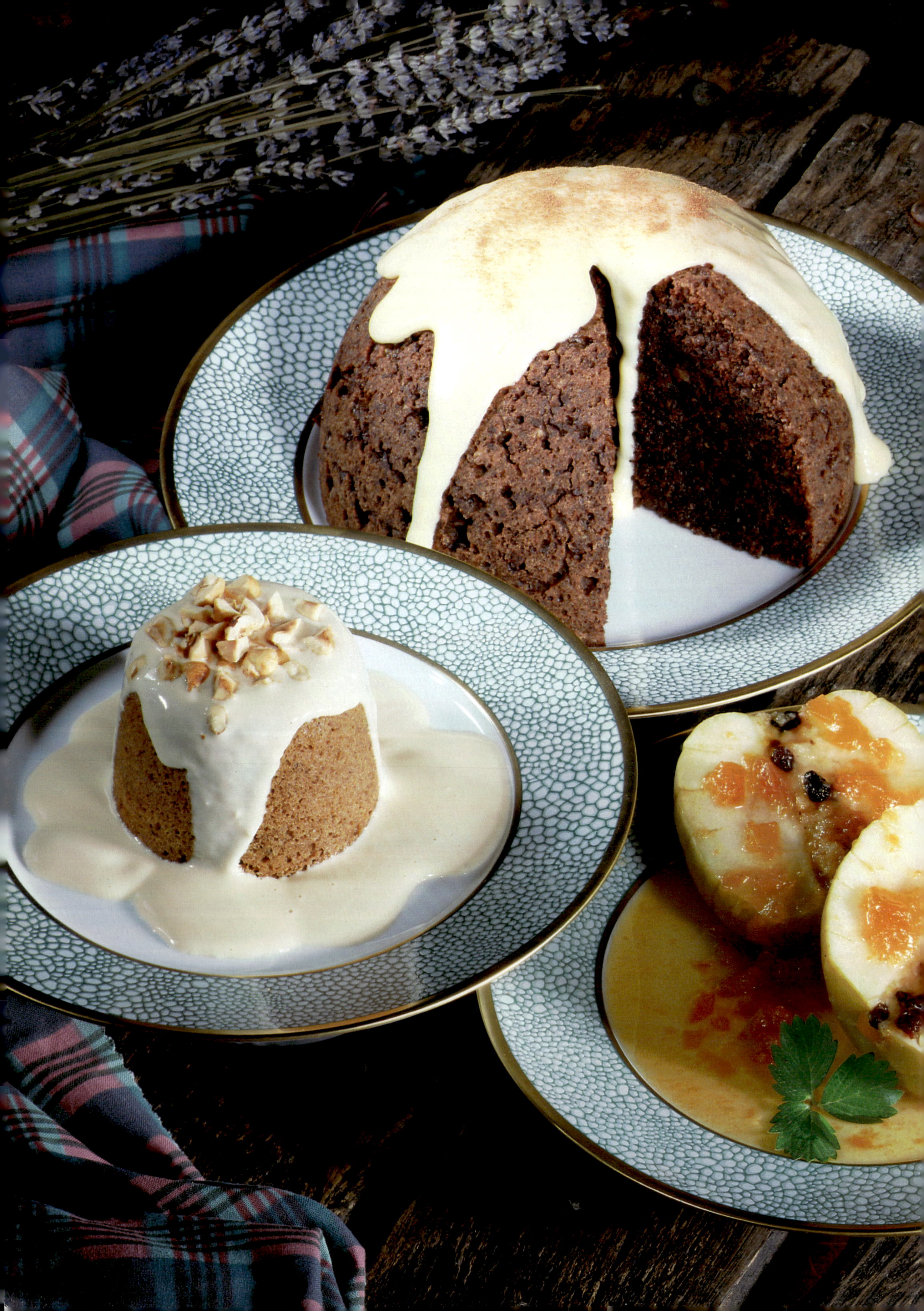

COFFEE AND HAZELNUT PUDDINGS

Kahlua is a coffee-flavoured liqueur. Recipe is best made just before serving. This recipe is not suitable to freeze or microwave.

½ cup self-raising flour
½ cup stale cake crumbs
½ cup packaged ground hazelnuts
4 eggs, separated
½ cup brown sugar
1 teaspoon vanilla essence
1 tablespoon dry instant coffee
1 tablespoon hot water
COFFEE LIQUEUR CREAM
½ cup cream
½ cup sour cream
2 teaspoons brown sugar
1 teaspoon vanilla essence
1 tablespoon Kahlua

Grease 6 moulds (1 cup capacity). Sift flour into medium bowl, stir in crumbs and nuts. Beat egg yolks, sugar and essence in small bowl with electric mixer until thick and creamy. Stir in combined coffee and water. Fold into flour mixture in 2 batches. Beat egg whites in small bowl with electric mixer until soft peaks form, fold lightly into pudding mixture.

Spoon mixture into prepared moulds, cover with greased rounds of paper, then foil, secure with string. Place moulds in baking dish, pour in enough boiling water to come halfway up sides of moulds. Bake in moderate oven for about 35 minutes or until firm. Serve with warm liqueur cream and chopped hazelnuts, if desired.
Coffee Liqueur Cream: Combine all ingredients in small saucepan, stir over heat until smooth.
Serves 6.

FRUITY BAKED APPLES AND APRICOT SAUCE

Apples are best baked just before serving. Sauce can be made a day ahead; keep, covered, in refrigerator. This recipe is not suitable to freeze.

6 medium apples, cored
½ cup packaged ground almonds
¼ cup castor sugar
1 teaspoon grated lemon rind
1 tablespoon currants
¼ teaspoon ground nutmeg
1 tablespoon chopped mixed peel
1 egg yolk
APRICOT SAUCE
½ cup chopped dried apricots
1 cup water
1 cup castor sugar

LEFT: Clockwise from top: Chocolate Bread Pudding with Brandy Cream, Fruity Baked Apples and Apricot Sauce, Coffee and Hazelnut Puddings.

Left: China and cutlery from Studio-Haus; fabric from Les Olivades

Mark around apple skins with sharp knife at 2cm intervals. Combine remaining ingredients in small bowl, push mixture into core cavities. Place apples into baking dish, cover with foil, bake in moderate oven for about 1 hour or until soft. Serve with warm apricot sauce.
Apricot Sauce: Combine apricots and water in small saucepan, bring to boil, reduce heat, simmer, uncovered, for about 5 minutes or until apricots are just soft, stir in sugar, stir over low heat until sugar is dissolved.
Serves 6.

CHOCOLATE BREAD PUDDING WITH BRANDY CREAM

Pudding can be made a day ahead; keep, covered, in refrigerator. Recipe unsuitable to freeze or microwave.

150g butter
¾ cup castor sugar
1 tablespoon brandy
5 eggs, lightly beaten
1¼ cups (150g) packaged ground almonds
375g dark chocolate, finely grated
2½ cups (250g) stale breadcrumbs
¼ cup cornflour
2 tablespoons cocoa
BRANDY CREAM
1½ cups milk
1 vanilla bean
4 egg yolks
⅓ cup castor sugar
1 teaspoon cornflour
2 tablespoons brandy

Grease pudding steamer (6 cup capacity). Beat butter, sugar and brandy in small bowl with electric mixer until light and fluffy. Add eggs gradually, beat well between additions. Mixture will curdle at this stage, but will reconstitute later. Transfer mixture to large bowl. Stir in almonds, chocolate, breadcrumbs and sifted cornflour and cocoa.

Pour mixture into prepared steamer, cover with greased round of paper, then foil, secure with string or lid. Place steamer in large saucepan with enough boiling water to come halfway up side of steamer; boil, covered, for about 2 hours or until firm. Stand pudding for 5 minutes before turning out. Serve hot pudding with brandy cream.
Brandy Cream: Combine milk and vanilla bean in small saucepan, bring to boil, reduce heat, simmer, uncovered, for 5 minutes. Remove from heat, cool, strain; wash bean, reserve for future use. Combine egg yolks, sugar and cornflour in top of double saucepan (or heatproof bowl), stir in milk, stir over simmering water until mixture is slightly thickened. Stir in brandy.

TANGERINE BRIOCHE WITH CREME ANGLAISE

You will need about 4 large tangerines for this recipe. Brioche can be made a day ahead; keep in airtight container. Reheat in moderate oven for about 5 minutes. Brioche can be frozen for 2 months. Crème anglaise can be made 2 days ahead; keep, covered, in refrigerator. This recipe is not suitable to microwave.

7g compressed yeast
1 tablespoon castor sugar
¼ cup warm milk
100g butter, melted
1 teaspoon grated tangerine rind
2 eggs, lightly beaten
2 cups plain flour
1 egg yolk, extra
1 tablespoon milk, extra

TANGERINE SYRUP
¼ cup castor sugar
¼ teaspoon grated tangerine rind
¼ cup tangerine juice

CREME ANGLAISE
2 tablespoons castor sugar
2 egg yolks
1 cup milk
1 tablespoon chopped tangerine rind
1 teaspoon cornflour
1 teaspoon custard powder
1 tablespoon water

Lightly oil 8 x 7cm fluted flan tins. Grate 1¼ teaspoons tangerine rind, chop 1 tablespoon rind finely. Squeeze ¼ cup juice. Segment remaining tangerines.

Cream yeast, sugar and milk in medium bowl, cover, stand in warm place for about 15 minutes or until frothy. Stir in butter, rind and eggs. Sift flour into large bowl, make well in centre, pour in egg mixture, mix to a soft sticky dough.

Turn dough onto lightly floured surface, knead for 5 minutes. Place dough in lightly greased large bowl, cover, stand in warm place for about 1 hour or until dough is doubled in size.

Turn dough onto lightly floured surface, knead for 1 minute. Divide dough into 8 portions, cut one-third of dough off each portion. Roll large portions into balls and place into prepared tins. Roll small portions into balls, place on top of each large ball. Push a skewer through both balls to bases of tins. Remove skewer. Cover brioche, stand in warm place for about 30 minutes or until doubled in size. Brush brioche lightly with combined extra egg yolk and extra milk. Bake in moderately hot oven for 10 minutes, reduce heat to moderate, bake further 10 minutes or until golden brown. Remove from oven, cool slightly, remove from tins.

Remove top knot from each brioche. Scoop out a little dough from the centre of each base, brush top and inside of brioche with tangerine syrup. Fill centre of each brioche with tangerine segments, replace top knot and serve with crème anglaise, dust with sifted icing sugar, if desired.

Tangerine Syrup: Combine sugar, rind and juice in small saucepan, stir over heat, without boiling, until sugar is dissolved, remove from heat; cool.

Crème Anglaise: Beat sugar and egg yolks in small bowl with electric mixer until thick and creamy. Combine milk and rind in medium saucepan, bring to boil, remove from heat, stir into egg mixture. Return mixture to saucepan, stir over heat, without boiling, until mixture thickens slightly. Blend cornflour and custard powder with water in small bowl, stir into milk mixture, stir over high heat until mixture boils and thickens.

Serves 8.

STEAMED PUMPKIN AND MAPLE PUDDING

You will need to cook 350g pumpkin for this recipe. Pudding can be made a day ahead; keep in airtight container. Pudding can be frozen for 2 months. Recipe unsuitable to microwave.

1 cup mashed cooked pumpkin
½ cup milk
90g butter, melted
2 eggs, lightly beaten
2 tablespoons honey
1 cup brown sugar, firmly packed
2 cups self-raising flour
1 teaspoon ground cinnamon
½ teaspoon ground nutmeg
½ cup slivered almonds
½ cup maple syrup

Grease pudding steamer (6 cup capacity) well. Combine pumpkin, milk, butter, eggs, honey and sugar in medium bowl; mix well. Stir in sifted dry ingredients and almonds. Pour into prepared steamer, cover with greased round of paper, then foil, secure with string or lid. Place steamer in large saucepan with enough boiling water to come halfway up side of steamer; boil, covered, for about 2 hours or until firm. Turn onto plate, serve with maple syrup and cream, if desired.

LEFT: Tangerine Brioche with Crème Anglaise.
RIGHT: Steamed Pumpkin and Maple Pudding.

Left: China from Villeroy & Boch

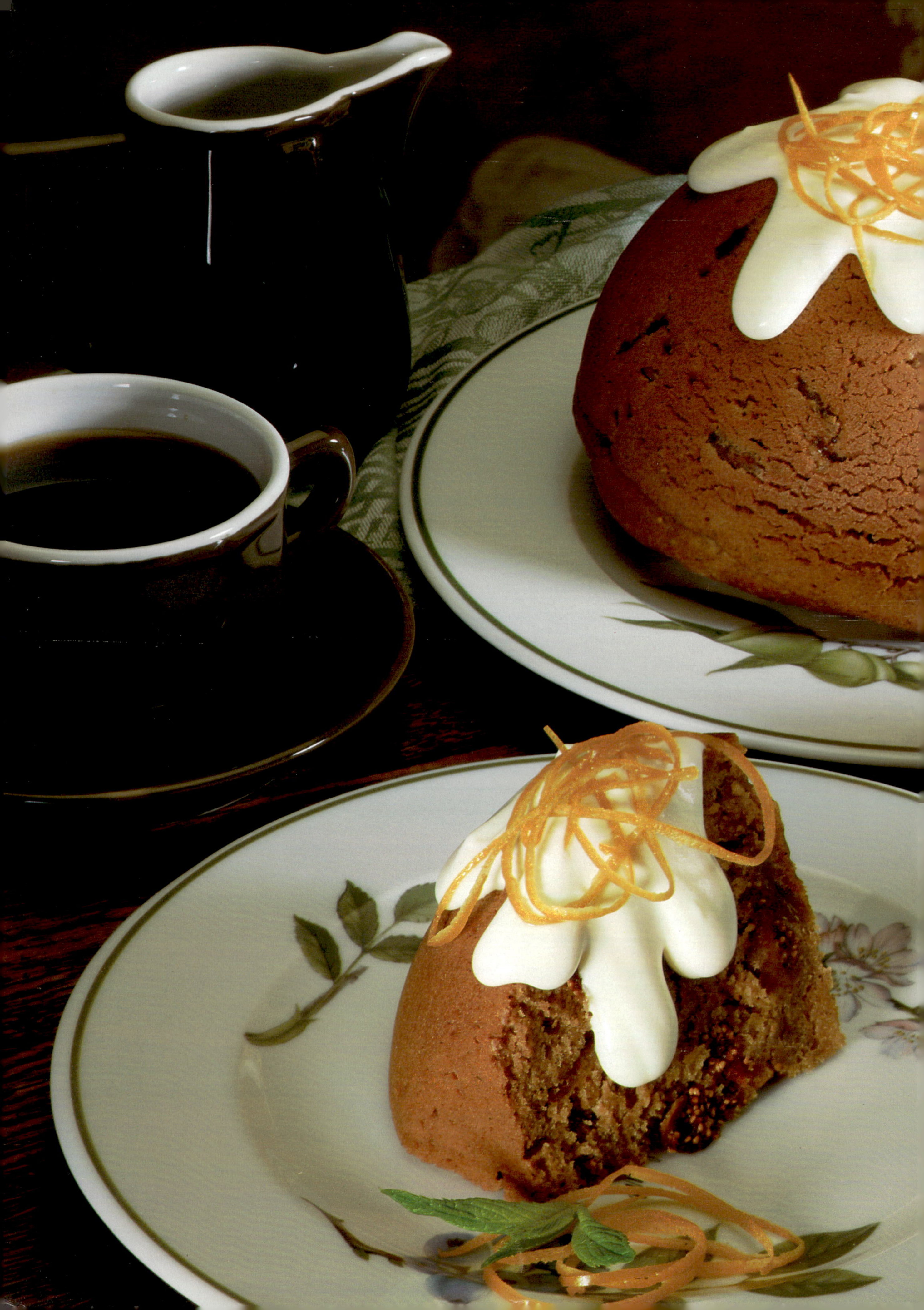

SPICY FIG AND GINGER PUDDING

Pudding is best made close to serving time, or can be frozen for 2 months. Recipe unsuitable to microwave.

¾ cup chopped dried figs
¼ cup chopped glacé ginger
60g butter
½ cup brown sugar
¼ cup water
1⅓ cups plain flour
1 teaspoon ground ginger
1 teaspoon mixed spice
¾ cup milk
1 tablespoon brown vinegar
1 teaspoon bicarbonate of soda

Grease pudding steamer well (6 cup capacity).

Combine figs, ginger, butter, sugar and water in medium saucepan, stir over heat until butter is melted; cool to room temperature.

Sift flour and spices into large bowl, make well in centre. Bring milk to boil in small saucepan, remove from heat, quickly stir in vinegar and sifted soda. Stir hot milk mixture and fig mixture into flour.

Pour mixture into prepared steamer, cover with greased round of paper, then foil, secure with string or lid. Place steamer in large saucepan with enough boiling water to come halfway up side of steamer; boil, covered, for about 1½ hours or until firm. Turn pudding onto serving plate, serve hot with extra whipped cream.

LEFT: Spicy Fig and Ginger Pudding.

Left: China and cloth from The Bay Tree

CHOCOLATE CHIP PUDDING

Pudding can be made a day ahead; keep, covered, in refrigerator or freeze for 3 months. This recipe is not suitable to microwave.

125g butter, chopped
2 teaspoons grated orange rind
1 cup castor sugar
4 eggs
½ cup packaged ground almonds
½ cup orange juice
½ cup stale cake crumbs
1 cup self-raising flour
1 cup plain flour
¾ cup Choc Bits
CHOCOLATE SAUCE
½ cup thickened cream
100g dark chocolate, chopped

Lightly grease pudding steamer (6 cup capacity).

Beat butter, rind and sugar in small bowl with electric mixer until light and fluffy. Beat in eggs, 1 at a time, beating well between additions. Mixture might curdle at this stage but will reconstitute later. Transfer mixture to large bowl. Stir in almonds, juice, crumbs and sifted flours in 2 batches, stir in Choc Bits.

Pour mixture into prepared steamer, cover with greased round of paper, then foil, secure with string or lid. Place steamer in large saucepan with enough boiling water to come halfway up side of steamer; boil, covered, for about 2 hours or until firm. Serve hot with sauce.

Chocolate Sauce: Combine cream and chocolate in small saucepan, stir over heat, without boiling, until mixture is smooth and heated through.

RIGHT: From top: Chocolate Chip Pudding, Black Forest Upside-Down Puddings.

Right: Plates from Woollahra Antiques; table from Appley Hoare Antiques.

BLACK FOREST UPSIDE-DOWN PUDDINGS

Puddings and sauce can be made several hours ahead; keep, covered, in refrigerator. This recipe is not suitable to freeze or microwave.

450g can pitted black cherries
1 tablespoon cornflour
75g dark chocolate, chopped
¼ cup boiling water
125g butter
1 cup castor sugar
2 eggs, separated
1¼ cups plain flour
½ teaspoon bicarbonate of soda
½ cup buttermilk
CUSTARD SAUCE
1 tablespoon cornflour
2 cups milk
2 eggs, lightly beaten
2 tablespoons castor sugar
1 teaspoon vanilla essence

Grease 6 moulds (1 cup capacity), line bases with paper, grease paper.

Drain cherries, reserve ½ cup syrup. Blend cornflour with 2 tablespoons of the syrup in small saucepan, stir in remaining syrup, stir over high heat until mixture boils and thickens. Remove from heat, cool to room temperature. Spread mixture evenly into moulds, top with cherries.

Combine chocolate and water in medium bowl, stir until chocolate is melted; cool to room temperature.

Beat butter, sugar and egg yolks in small bowl with electric mixer until light and fluffy. Transfer mixture to large bowl, stir in chocolate mixture, then sifted flour, soda and buttermilk in 2 batches. Beat egg whites in small bowl with electric mixer until soft peaks form, fold into chocolate mixture.

Spoon pudding mixture into moulds, cover with greased rounds of paper, then foil, secure with string. Place moulds in baking dish, pour in enough boiling water to come halfway up sides of moulds. Bake in moderate oven for about 45 minutes or until firm, turn onto plates, serve warm with sauce.

Custard Sauce: Blend cornflour and 2 tablespoons of the milk in small saucepan, stir in remaining milk, stir over high heat until mixture boils and thickens. Remove from heat, beat in combined eggs, sugar and essence.

Serves 6.

GINGER WAFFLES WITH PECAN SAUCE

Waffles and sauce are best made just before serving. Cooked waffles can be frozen for 2 months. This recipe is not suitable to microwave.

¼ cup golden syrup
¼ cup water
2 tablespoons brown sugar
60g butter
1 egg, separated
¾ cup plain flour
1½ tablespoons ground ginger
½ teaspoon ground cinnamon
½ teaspoon ground nutmeg
½ teaspoon bicarbonate of soda

PECAN SAUCE
½ cup castor sugar
¼ cup water
½ cup thickened cream
45g butter
¼ cup chopped pecans
pinch ground cinnamon

Combine golden syrup, water, sugar and butter in medium saucepan, stir over heat, without boiling, until sugar is dissolved. Bring to boil, remove from heat; cool to room temperature, stir in egg yolk. Stir in sifted flour, ginger, cinnamon, nutmeg and soda in 2 batches; mix to a smooth batter. Beat egg white in small bowl until soft peaks form, fold into batter. Drop about 2 tablespoons of mixture onto heated greased waffle iron. Close iron, cook for about 2 minutes or until golden brown. Repeat with remaining batter. Serve waffles with warm pecan sauce and ice cream, if desired.

Pecan Sauce: Combine sugar and water in medium saucepan, stir over heat, without boiling, until sugar is dissolved, bring to boil, boil, without stirring, until golden brown. Carefully add cream to pan (the cream will bubble quite fiercely and mixture will harden). Stir over heat until toffee is melted. Remove from heat, stir in butter, nuts and cinnamon.

Serves 4.

LEMON PASSIONFRUIT DELICIOUS

You will need about 5 medium passionfruit for this recipe. Pudding is best made just before serving. This recipe is not suitable to freeze or microwave.

**4 eggs, separated
½ cup castor sugar
30g butter, melted
½ cup milk
½ cup passionfruit pulp
¼ cup water
⅔ cup self-raising flour
¼ cup lemon juice
½ cup castor sugar, extra**

Grease ovenproof dish (4 cup capacity). Beat egg yolks and sugar in small bowl with electric mixer until thick and creamy. Transfer to large bowl. Stir in butter, milk, passionfruit, water, sifted flour and juice.

Beat egg whites in small bowl with electric mixer until soft peaks form, gradually add extra sugar, beat until dissolved between additions. Fold egg white mixture into lemon mixture, pour into prepared dish. Place in baking dish, pour in enough boiling water to come halfway up side of dish. Bake in moderate oven for about 45 minutes or until firm. Stand 5 minutes before serving. Dust with sifted icing sugar, if desired.

Serves 6.

ABOVE LEFT: Ginger Waffles with Pecan Sauce.
ABOVE: Lemon Passionfruit Delicious.

Above left: Cutlery from The Bay Tree

GINGER AND ORANGE SELF-SAUCING PUDDING

Pudding is best made just before serving. This recipe is not suitable to freeze or microwave.

90g butter
2 teaspoons grated orange rind
⅓ cup brown sugar
¼ cup golden syrup
1 egg
1 tablespoon chopped glacé ginger
1 cup self-raising flour
2 teaspoons ground ginger
½ cup milk
¼ cup castor sugar
1 teaspoon cornflour
1 cup green ginger wine

Grease ovenproof dish (4 cup capacity). Beat butter, rind, brown sugar and golden syrup in small bowl with electric mixer until light and fluffy; beat in egg. Stir in glacé ginger, sifted flour and ground ginger with milk in 2 batches. Pour mixture into prepared dish.

Blend castor sugar and cornflour with 1 tablespoon of the wine in small saucepan, stir in remaining wine. Stir over high heat until mixture boils and thickens, pour gently over mixture in dish. Bake in moderately hot oven for about 1 hour or until firm. Stand 5 minutes before serving. Dust with sifted icing sugar, if desired.

Serves 6.

PINEAPPLE SELF-SAUCING PUDDING

Pudding is best made just before serving. This recipe is not suitable to freeze or microwave.

30g butter
2 teaspoons grated lemon rind
½ cup castor sugar
3 eggs, separated
2 tablespoons self-raising flour
1 cup milk
½ cup coconut
450g can crushed pineapple, drained

Grease ovenproof dish (4 cup capacity). Beat butter, rind, sugar and egg yolks in small bowl with electric mixer until thick and creamy. Transfer to larger bowl. Stir in sifted flour, milk and coconut in 2 batches. Stir in pineapple.

Beat egg whites in small bowl with electric mixer until soft peaks form, fold into pineapple mixture. Pour mixture into prepared dish. Bake in moderate oven for about 40 minutes or until firm. Stand 5 minutes before serving. Dust with sifted icing sugar, if desired.

Serves 6.

COFFEE FUDGE SELF-SAUCING PUDDING

Pudding is best made close to serving time. Recipe unsuitable to freeze.

½ cup milk
2 tablespoons dry instant coffee
1 cup self-raising flour
½ cup castor sugar
½ cup brown sugar
1 egg, lightly beaten
30g butter, melted
COFFEE FUDGE SAUCE
2 cups water
2 tablespoons dry instant coffee
¾ cup brown sugar, lightly packed
3 teaspoons golden syrup
45g butter, melted

Grease ovenproof dish (8 cup capacity). Heat milk and coffee in small saucepan until coffee is dissolved; cool. Sift flour and sugars into large bowl, make well in centre. Stir in combined egg, butter and milk coffee mixture.

Pour mixture into prepared dish. Carefully pour coffee fudge sauce over mixture. Bake in moderate oven for about 1 hour (or microwave on HIGH for about 12 minutes) or until pudding is firm, stand 5 minutes before serving. Dust with sifted icing sugar, if desired.

Coffee Fudge Sauce: Combine all ingredients in large jug; mix well.

Serves 6.

RIGHT: Clockwise from top: Ginger and Orange Self-Saucing Pudding, Pineapple Self-Saucing Pudding, Coffee Fudge Self-Saucing Pudding.

Bowls from Accoutrement

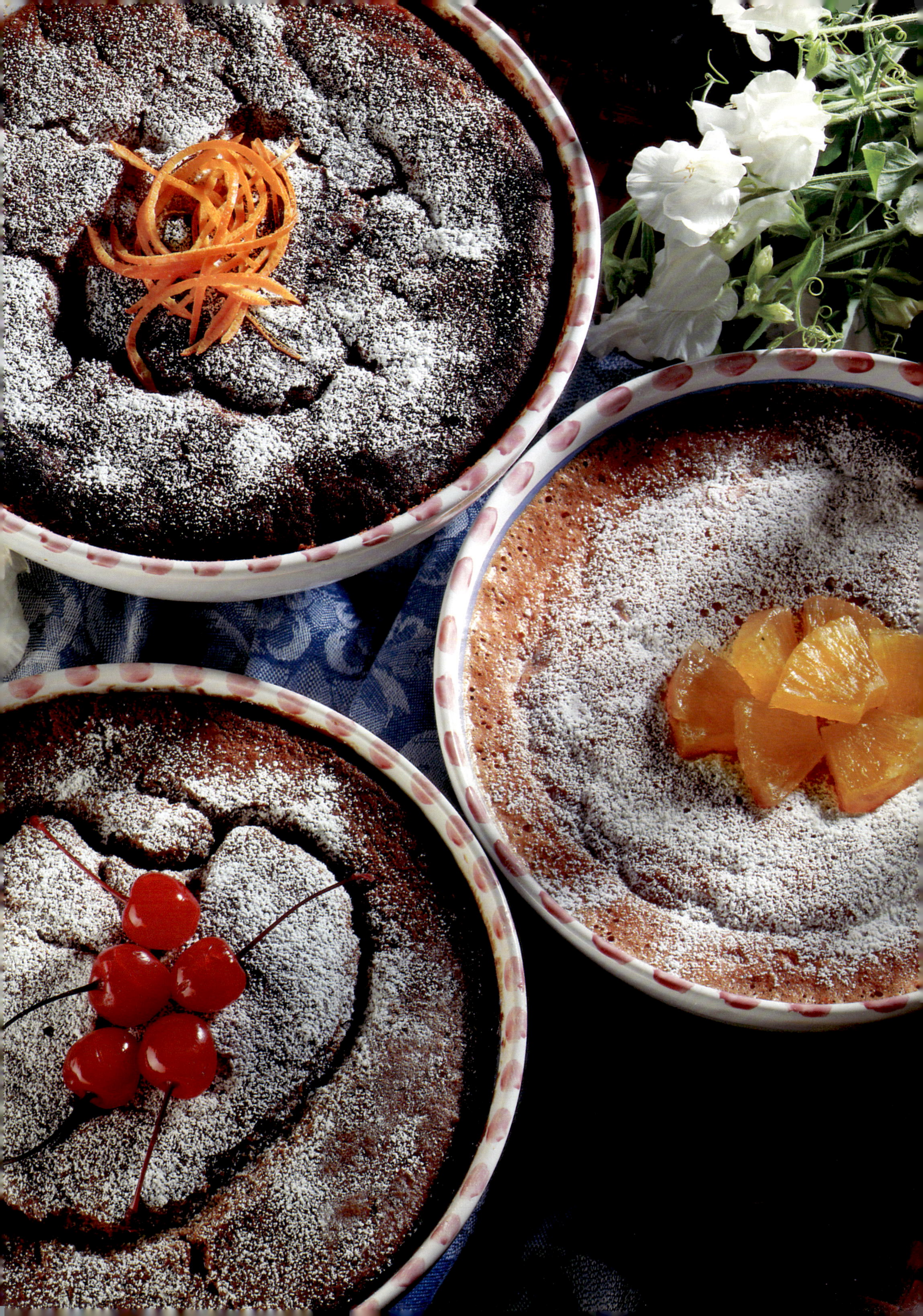

HAZELNUT BUTTERSCOTCH SELF-SAUCING PUDDING

Recipe is best made just before serving. This recipe is not suitable to freeze or microwave.

- ¾ cup self-raising flour
- ¼ cup packaged ground hazelnuts
- 400g can sweetened condensed milk
- 30g butter
- 1 teaspoon vanilla essence
- ½ cup milk
- 1 cup brown sugar, firmly packed
- 1¾ cups boiling water

Grease ovenproof dish (8 cup capacity). Sift flour into medium bowl, stir in hazelnuts. Place condensed milk into small heavy-based saucepan, stir over medium heat for about 10 minutes or until thickened slightly and pale golden brown. Stir in butter, essence and milk, stir until butter is melted; stand until warm. Pour milk mixture into flour mixture; mix well.

Pour mixture into prepared dish. Sift brown sugar over top of pudding mixture, carefully pour water evenly over top of pudding. Bake in moderate oven for about 35 minutes or until firm. Stand 5 minutes before serving. Dust with sifted icing sugar, if desired.

Serves 6.

BELOW: Hazelnut Butterscotch Self-Saucing Pudding.

QUICK CARAMEL SAUCE

Sauce can be made 2 days ahead; keep, covered, in refrigerator. This recipe is not suitable to freeze.

30g butter
200g packet Jersey caramels
2 x 100g packets white marshmallows
300ml carton thickened cream
1 teaspoon vanilla essence

Combine butter, caramels and marshmallows in medium saucepan, stir over heat, without boiling, until caramels and marshmallows are melted (or microwave on HIGH for about 2 minutes). Stir in cream and essence. Stir over medium heat (or microwave on HIGH for about 2 minutes) until mixture boils. Serve warm or cold.

Makes about 3 cups.

APRICOT AND RUM SAUCE

Sauce can be made a day ahead; keep, covered, in refrigerator. This recipe is not suitable to freeze.

¾ cup apricot nectar
420g can apricot halves
¼ cup castor sugar
1 tablespoon cornflour
½ cup thickened cream
1 tablespoon white rum

Blend or process nectar and undrained apricots until smooth. Blend sugar and cornflour with apricot mixture in medium saucepan until smooth. Stir over high heat until sauce boils and thickens slightly. Stir in cream and rum. Serve warm or cold.

Makes about 3 cups.

ABOVE: From left: Quick Caramel Sauce, Apricot and Rum Sauce.

Above: Jugs from The Australian East India Co.; fabric from Derek Scott

MELBA SAUCE

Sauce can be made 3 days ahead; keep, covered, in refrigerator or freeze for 3 months. This recipe is not suitable to microwave.

450g can sliced peaches
200g punnet raspberries
½ cup castor sugar
1 tablespoon cornflour
¼ cup brandy

Drain peaches; reserve ⅔ cup syrup. Blend or process berries and peaches until smooth; strain, discard seeds. Pour mixture into medium saucepan, add sugar, stir over heat, without boiling, until sugar is dissolved. Blend cornflour with reserved syrup in small bowl, stir into berry mixture, stir over high heat until mixture boils and thickens. Stir in brandy. Serve warm or cold.
    Makes about 2 cups.

ROCKY ROAD SAUCE

Sauce is best made just before serving. Recipe unsuitable to freeze.

200g dark chocolate, melted
½ cup cream, warmed
¾ cup packaged white marshmallows, chopped
¼ cup chopped red glacé cherries
¼ cup crushed mixed nuts

Combine chocolate and cream in bowl; stir in remaining ingredients; mix well.
    Makes about 2 cups.

MOCHA LIQUEUR SAUCE

Tia Maria is a coffee-flavoured liqueur. Sauce is best prepared close to serving time. This recipe is not suitable to freeze or microwave.

6 egg yolks
¼ cup castor sugar
2 teaspoons vanilla essence
2 x 300ml cartons thickened cream
2 teaspoons dry instant coffee
½ cup hot water
2 tablespoons Tia Maria
2 tablespoons chocolate topping

Combine egg yolks, sugar and essence in top of double saucepan (or in heatproof bowl), beat with electric mixer until thick and creamy. Bring cream to boil in medium saucepan, stir into egg mixture, stir over simmering water until mixture coats back of spoon. Stir in combined coffee and water, liqueur and topping. Serve warm.
    Makes (1 litre) 4 cups.

RIGHT: Clockwise from back: Melba Sauce, Rocky Road Sauce, Mocha Liqueur Sauce.

Fabric from Les Olivades

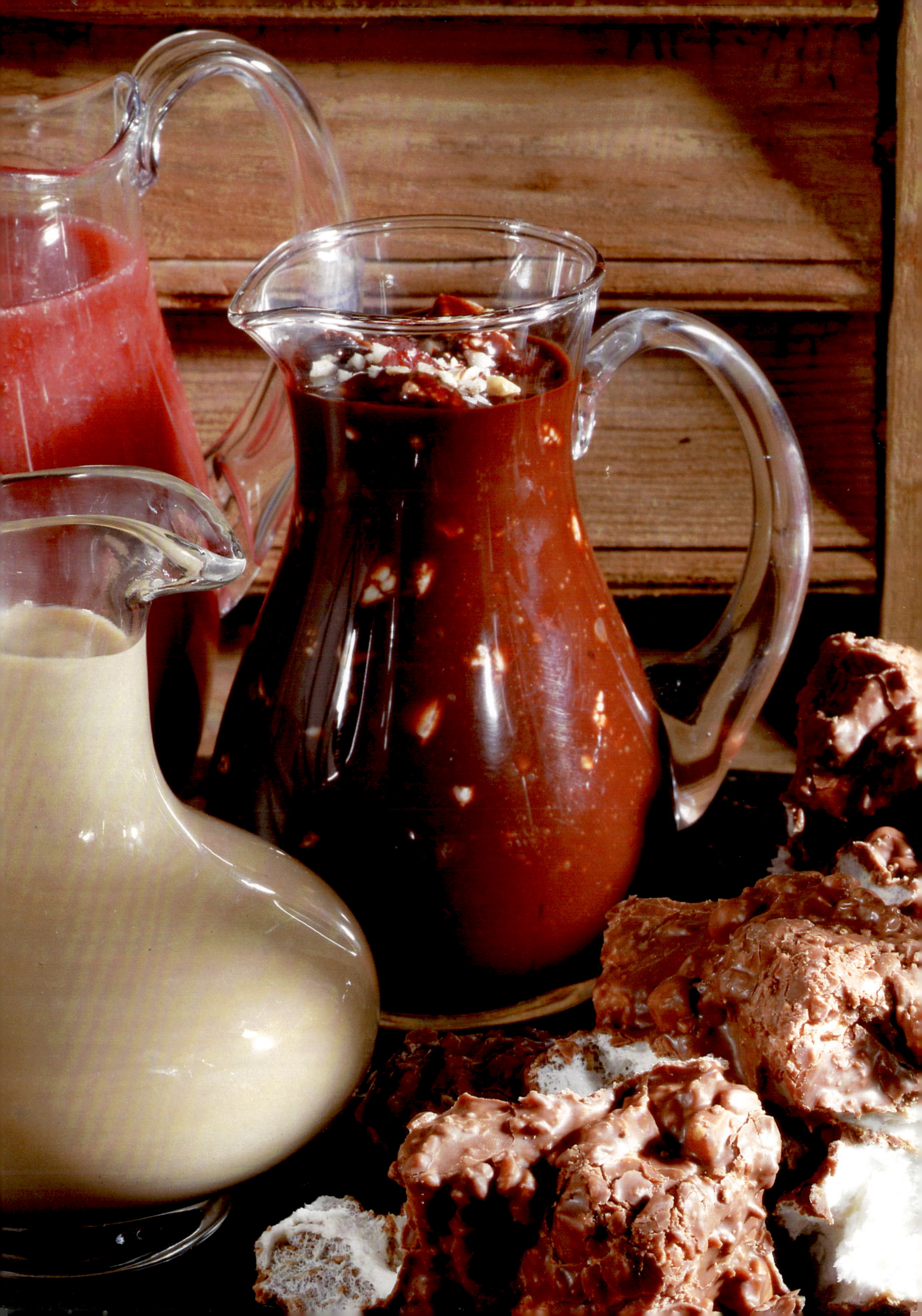

PASSIONFRUIT MINT SAUCE

You will need about 8 passionfruit for this recipe. Sauce can be made 3 days ahead; keep, covered, in refrigerator. This recipe is not suitable to freeze.

BELOW: Passionfruit Mint Sauce.

1½ tablespoons cornflour
1 cup water
½ cup passionfruit pulp
1½ tablespoons chopped fresh mint
2 tablespoons dry white wine
⅓ cup castor sugar
2 tablespoons passionfruit pulp, extra
½ teaspoon chopped fresh mint, extra

Blend cornflour with 2 tablespoons of the water in medium saucepan. Stir in remaining water, passionfruit, mint, wine and sugar, stir over high heat (or microwave on HIGH for about 3 minutes) until mixture boils and thickens, strain; cool. Stir in extra passionfruit and extra mint.

Makes about 1 cup.

GLOSSARY

Some terms, names and alternatives are included here to help everyone to understand and use our recipes perfectly.

ARROWROOT: a thickening ingredient. Cornflour can be used as a substitute.

BAKING POWDER: can be made in the proportion of ½ teaspoon bicarbonate of soda to 1 teaspoon cream of tartar. This is equivalent to 2 teaspoons baking powder. Sift ingredients together several times before using.

BICARBONATE OF SODA: baking soda; a component of baking powder.

BREADCRUMBS: Stale: use 1- and 2-day-old bread made into crumbs by grating, blending or processing. **Packaged:** use commercially-packaged breadcrumbs.

BUTTER: we used salted butter unless otherwise specified; a good-quality cooking margarine can be used, if preferred.

BUTTERMILK: made by adding a culture to skim milk to give a slightly acid flavour. Skim milk can be substituted, if preferred.

CHESTNUT SPREAD: sweetened purée of chestnuts.

CHOC MELTS: discs of dark compounded chocolate; ideal for melting and moulding.

CHOCOLATE: Dark Chocolate: we used dark eating chocolate available in 50g, 200g and 250g blocks. **Milk Chocolate:** available in 50g, 200g and 250g blocks.

COCONUT CREAM: is available in cans and cartons in supermarkets and Asian stores; coconut milk can be substituted although it is not as thick. To make coconut milk; place 2 cups of desiccated coconut in large bowl, cover with 2½ cups of hot water, cover, stand until mixture is just warm. Mix by hand, then strain through a fine sieve or cloth, squeezing out as much liquid as you can. This will give you about 1½ cups of thick milk.

COCONUT MACAROONS: crisp biscuits made from coconut, sugar and egg whites.

COLOURINGS: we used concentrated liquid vegetable food colourings.

CORNFLOUR: cornstarch.

CREAM: we have specified thickened (whipping) cream when necessary in recipes. Cream refers to light pouring cream, also known as half 'n' half. **Sour Cream:** a thick commercially-cultured sour cream.

CUMQUATS: orange-coloured citrus fruit about the size of walnuts. Usually preserved or used for making jam, the skin is always retained.

CUSTARD APPLE: cherimoya.

DARK RUM: we prefer to use an underproof rum (not overproof) for a more subtle flavour.

ESSENCE: extract.

FLOUR: Plain Flour: all-purpose flour. **Self-Raising Flour:** substitute plain (all-purpose) flour and baking powder in the proportion of ¾ metric cup plain flour to 2 level metric teaspoons baking powder; sift together several times. If using an 8oz measuring cup, use 1 cup plain flour to 2 level metric teaspoons baking powder. **Wholemeal Plain Flour:** wholewheat all-purpose flour. **Wholemeal Self-Raising Flour:** add baking powder as indicated above to wholewheat all-purpose flour.

GLACE GINGER: crystallised ginger can be substituted for glacé ginger; rinse off the sugar with warm water, dry ginger well before using.

GOLDEN SYRUP: maple syrup, pancake syrup or honey can be substituted.

GREEN GINGER WINE: an Australian sweet wine infused with ginger. It has an alcohol content of 17 percent.

INSTANT PUDDING MIX: a blancmange-style dessert mix.

KIWI FRUIT: Chinese gooseberry.

LEMON BUTTER: lemon curd or lemon cheese.

LIGHT CORN SYRUP: an imported product available from supermarkets, delicatessens and health food stores. It is also available in dark — either can be substituted for the other.

LOW FAT COTTAGE CHEESE: contains less than 4 percent fat.

MARSALA: a sweet, fortified wine, traditionally from Italy.

PACKAGED NUTS: we used packaged commercially-ground and whole nuts in our recipes unless otherwise specified.

PUNNET: basket usually holding about 250g of fruit.

RICOTTA CHEESE: we used cheese with 10 percent fat content.

RIND: zest.

ROCKMELON: cantaloupe

ROSEWATER: an extract of rose petals, used to flavour sweet dishes, creams, cakes and puddings. Available from Asian stores and some health stores.

SAVARIN PAN: a ring cake pan with a rounded base.

SEMOLINA: a cereal made from the endosperm of hard durum wheat. Used in puddings, cakes, desserts and some savoury dishes.

SUGAR: Brown: a soft fine sugar with some molasses present which gives its characteristic appearance and flavour. **Castor:** fine, granulated table or berry sugar. **Crystal:** use a coarse, granulated table sugar. **Icing:** confectioners' or powdered sugar. We used icing sugar mixture (not pure) in the recipes in this book. **Raw:** natural brown granulated sugar or "sugar in the raw" can be used.

SWEETENED CONDENSED MILK: we used milk from which 60 percent of the water has been removed; the remaining milk is then sweetened.

TANGELO: a cross between grapefruit and tangerine. It is eaten like an orange.

TANGERINE: citrus fruit similar to a mandarin. It is bright orange to red.

VANILLA BEAN: dried bean of the vanilla orchid. Used as a flavouring for pudding, cakes, creams, etc. It can be used repeatedly, simply wash in warm water after use, dry well and store in airtight container.

VANILLA ESSENCE: we used imitation essence.

WALNUT OIL: oil pressed from ground walnuts.

YEAST: allow 3 teaspoons (7g) dried granulated yeast to 15g compressed (fresh) yeast.

Cup and Spoon Measurements

To ensure accuracy in your recipes use the standard metric measuring equipment approved by Standards Australia:
(a) 250 millilitre cup for measuring liquids. A litre jug *(capacity 4 cups)* is also available.
(b) a graduated set of four cups — measuring 1 cup, half, third and quarter cup — for items such as flour, sugar, etc. When measuring in these fractional cups, level off at the brim.
(c) a graduated set of four spoons: tablespoon *(20 millilitre liquid capacity)*, teaspoon *(5 millilitre)*, half and quarter teaspoons. The Australian, British and American teaspoon each has 5ml capacity.

Approximate cup and spoon conversion chart

Australian	American & British
1 cup	1¼ cups
¾ cup	1 cup
⅔ cup	¾ cup
½ cup	⅔ cup
⅓ cup	½ cup
¼ cup	⅓ cup
2 tablespoons	¼ cup
1 tablespoon	4 teaspoons

Oven Temperatures

Electric	C°	F°
Very slow	120	250
Slow	150	300
Moderately slow	160-180	325-350
Moderate	180-200	375-400
Moderately hot	210-230	425-450
Hot	240-250	475-500
Very hot	260	525-550

Gas	C°	F°
Very slow	120	250
Slow	150	300
Moderately slow	160	325
Moderate	180	350
Moderately hot	190	375
Hot	200	400
Very hot	230	450

We have used large eggs with an average weight of 60g each in all recipes.
ALL SPOON MEASUREMENTS ARE LEVEL.
Note: NZ, Canada, USA and UK all use 15ml tablespoons.

INDEX

A

Almond Custard with Plum Sauce, Fried	72
Almond Custard, Nougat	70
Almond Pithivier, Apricot	82
Almond Tartlets, Tamarillo	85
Apple Cobbler, Rhubarb and	102
Apple Fritters with Praline Butter	94
Apple Souffles, Fresh	96
Apple Tarte Tatin	91
Apples and Apricot Sauce, Fruity Baked	109
Apples with Cinnamon Custard, Pastry	90
Apricot Almond Pithivier	82
Apricot and Rum Sauce	121
Apricot Ice Cream with Choc Coconut Sauce	38
Apricot Souffle Crepes	79
Apricot Trifle, Brandied	71

B

Baked Apples and Apricot Sauce, Fruity	109
Baked Lemon Sour Cream Cheesecake	56
Banana Coconut Pancakes	74
Bananas with Peanut Caramel Cream	13
Bavarian, Lime and Jelly	26
Berry Moulds with Fruit Sauce	8
Berry Parfaits, Chantilly	2
Black Forest Upside-Down Puddings	115
Black Forest Crepes	75
Blancmange, Coffee Liqueur	8
Blueberry Delights with Orange Liqueur Cream	11
Bombe, Marbled Strawberry	54
Boysenberry Fillo Flan	87
Brandied Apricot Trifle	71
Brioche with Creme Anglaise, Tangerine	110
Brownies with Raspberry Sauce, Chocolate	101
Buttermilk Pancakes with Spicy Apple	75
Butterscotch Rum Moulds	45
Butterscotch Self-Saucing Pudding, Hazelnut	120

C

CAKES

Chocolate Mallow Roll with Raspberry Sauce	67
Coconut Roulade with Cherry Cream	66
Coffee Gateau with Tangerine Cream	65
Cumquat Layer	63
Layered Ricotta Chocolate	64
Pecan Pumpkin with Cinnamon Cream	66
Caramel Cream, Bananas with Peanut	13
Caramel Sauce, Quick	121
Caramel Souffles with Walnut Praline	29
Cardamom Ice Cream with Macadamia Tuiles	40
Cassata Bombe, Frozen	41
Champagne Jelly, Peachy	3
Chantilly Berry Parfaits	2

CHEESECAKES

Baked Lemon Sour Cream	56
Chocolate Rum	60
Cumquat Liqueur	59
Jelly Crunch	61
Passionfruit Ginger	56
Plum with Toffee	59
Cherry Fritters with Two Sauces	93
Cherry Turnovers, Orange Glazed	90
Chestnut Cases with Strawberry Sauce, Chocolate	20
Chocolate Bags with Cherry Liqueur Cream	17
Chocolate Bread Pudding with Brandy Cream	109
Chocolate Brownies with Raspberry Sauce	101
Chocolate Chestnut Cases with Strawberry Sauce	20
Chocolate Chip Pudding	114
Chocolate Fudge Fritters	92
Chocolate Hazelnut Meringue	53
Chocolate Liqueur Souffles	100
Chocolate Mallow Roll with Raspberry Sauce	67
Chocolate Orange Cups	7
Chocolate Pancakes with Mint Cream	78
Chocolate Rum Cheesecake	60
Clafouti, Plum	104
Classic Pavlova	53
Cobbler, Rhubarb and Apple	102
Coconut Bake, Lime	68
Coconut Roulade with Cherry Cream	66
Coconut Savarin with Cumquats	105
Coconut Snap Horns with Cardamom Cream	18
Coconut Yogurt, Custard Apple	23
Coffee and Hazelnut Puddings	109
Coffee Creme Caramels	72
Coffee Fudge Self-Saucing Pudding	118
Coffee Gateau with Tangerine Cream	65
Coffee Liqueur Blancmange	8
Coffee Souffles with Pecan Praline Cream	96
Compote with Champagne, Mandarin	11
Cream Hearts with Berry Sauce	21
Creamy Lemon Crumble	72
Creamy Marsala Souffles	31
Creme Caramels, Coffee	72
Creme Caramels, Ginger	71

CREPES

Apricot Souffle	79
Black Forest	75
Mandarin with Mandarin Syrup	77
Orange with Coffee Liqueur Sauce	79
Tropical Flambe	78
Crumble, Creamy Lemon	72
Cumquat Layer Cake	63
Cumquat Liqueur Cheesecake	59
Cumquat Syllabub	17
Cumquats, Coconut Savarin with	105
Custard Apple and Passionfruit Flan	15
Custard Apple Coconut Yogurt	23
Custard Apple Fruit Salad	18

CUSTARD

Coffee Creme Caramels	72
Fried Almond with Plum Sauce	72
Ginger Creme Caramels	71
Lime Coconut Bake	68
Nougat Almond	70
Passionfruit Creams	68

D

Date Fritters with Lemon Sauce, Spicy	95
Delicious, Lemon Passionfruit	117
Double Chocolate Snowballs	4
Dumplings in Honey Syrup, Pecan	102
Dumplings, Mandarin Syrup	107

F

Fig and Ginger Pudding, Spicy	113
Fillo Flan, Boysenberry	87
Flan, Boysenberry Fillo	87
Flan, Custard Apple and Passionfruit	15
Flan, Golden Carrot	84
Fresh Apple Souffles	96
Fresh Tangerine Jelly	4
Fried Almond Custard with Plum Sauce	72

FRITTERS

Apple with Praline Butter	94
Cherry with Two Sauces	93
Chocolate Fudge	92
Semolina with Almond Liqueur Syrup	94
Spicy Date with Lemon Sauce	95
Toffee Pear	92
Frozen Cassata Bombe	41

FRUIT

Bananas with Peanut Caramel Cream	13
Berry Moulds with Fruit Sauce	8
Blueberry Delights with Orange Liqueur Cream	11
Chantilly Berry Parfaits	2
Cherry Fritters with Two Sauces	93
Coconut Savarin with Cumquats	105
Custard Apple Fruit Salad	18
Fruit Salad Ring	23
Fruity Baked Apples and Apricot Sauce	109
Island Fruits with Liqueur Cream	4
Macaroon Peaches	103
Mandarin Compote with Champagne	11
Mandarins Jubilee	18
Mango Creams	23
Pastry Apples with Cinnamon Custard	90
Plum Clafouti	104
Poached Pears with Orange Liqueur Sauce	104
Rhubarb and Apple Cobbler	102
Spicy Date Fritters with Lemon Sauce	95
Toffee Lattice with Fresh Fruit	24
Toffee Pear Fritters	92
Fruit Salad Ring	23
Fruit Salad, Custard Apple	18
Fruits with Liqueur Cream, Island	2
Fruity Baked Apples and Apricot Sauce	109

G

Gateau Saint Honore with Raspberry Cream	82
Gateau with Tangerine Cream, Coffee	65
Ginger and Orange Self-Saucing Pudding	118
Ginger and Peach Mousse, Glace	26
Ginger Creme Caramels	71
Ginger Pudding, Spicy Fig and	113
Ginger Souffles	99
Ginger Waffles with Pecan Sauce	116
Gingerbread Ice Cream, Walnut	40
Glace Ginger and Peach Mousse	26
Golden Carrot Flan	84

H

Hazelnut Butterscotch Self-Saucing Pudding	120
Hazelnut Meringue, Chocolate	53
Hazelnut Puddings, Coffee and	109
Hazelnut Tart, Pear and	82
Horns with Cardamom Cream, Coconut Snap	18

I

Ice Cream Puffs with Tamarillo Sauce	80

ICE CREAMS

Apricot with Choc Coconut Sauce	38
Butterscotch Rum Moulds	45
Cardamom with Macadamia Tuiles	40
Frozen Cassata Bombe	41
Licorice	44
Lime	38
Lime and Pear with Poached Pears	37
Maraschino Ice Cream Cake	43
Peachy Ice Cream Swans	49
Pumpkin and Maple	39
Strawberry Parfait	42
Walnut Gingerbread	40
Ice, Orange and Mango	39
Island Fruits with Liqueur Cream	2

127

J

JELLIES
- Blueberry Delights with Orange Liqueur Cream — 11
- Fresh Tangerine — 4
- Peachy Champagne — 3
- Jelly Crunch Cheesecake — 61

L

- Layered Pink Sorbet Terrine — 47
- Layered Ricotta Chocolate Cake — 64
- Leaf Vol au Vents with Mango Cream — 88
- Lemon Crumble, Creamy — 72
- Lemon Passionfruit Delicious — 117
- Lemon Sour Cream Cheesecake, Baked — 56
- Licorice Ice Cream — 44
- Lime and Jelly Bavarian — 26
- Lime and Mint Sorbet — 36
- Lime and Pear Ice Cream with Poached Pears — 37
- Lime Coconut Bake — 68
- Lime Ice Cream — 38
- Liqueur Sauce, Mocha — 122

M

- Macadamia Tuiles, Cardamom Ice Cream with — 40
- Macaroon Peaches — 103
- Mandarin Compote with Champagne — 11
- Mandarin Crepes with Mandarin Syrup — 77
- Mandarin Syrup Dumplings — 107
- Mandarins Jubilee — 18
- Mango Creams — 23
- Mango Ice, Orange and — 39
- Mango Souffles with Chocolate Collars — 33
- Maple Ice Cream, Pumpkin and — 39
- Maple Pudding, Steamed Pumpkin and — 111
- Maraschino Ice Cream Cake with Strawberry Coulis — 42
- Marbled Strawberry Bombe — 54
- Marsala Souffles, Creamy — 31
- Melba Sauce — 122

MERINGUES
- Chocolate Hazelnut — 53
- Classic Pavlova — 53
- Kisses with Passionfruit Glaze — 48
- Marbled Strawberry Bombe — 54
- Mocha Triangles — 50
- Peachy Ice Cream Swans — 49
- Tangerine Cups — 52
- Terrine with Chocolate Sauce — 56

- Meringue Kisses with Passionfruit Glaze — 48
- Meringue Terrine with Chocolate Sauce — 56
- Mint Sauce, Passionfruit — 124
- Mint Sorbet, Lime and — 36
- Mocha Liqueur Sauce — 122
- Mocha Meringue Triangles — 50

MOUSSES
- Glace Ginger and Peach — 27
- Lime and Jelly Bavarian — 26
- Pina Colada — 30
- Spicy Pumpkin and Hazelnut — 34
- Strawberry with Tropical Sauce — 26

N, O

- Nougat Almond Custard — 70
- Orange and Mango Ice — 39
- Orange Crepes with Coffee Liqueur Sauce — 79
- Orange Cups, Chocolate — 7
- Orange Glazed Cherry Turnovers — 90
- Orange Liqueur Souffles with Macerated Fruits — 99

P, Q

PANCAKES
- Banana Coconut — 74
- Buttermilk with Spicy Apple — 75
- Chocolate with Mint Cream — 78

- Parfaits, Chantilly Berry — 2
- Paris-Brest, Tangerine — 80
- Passionfruit Mint Sauce — 124
- Passionfruit Creams — 68
- Passionfruit Delicious, Lemon — 117
- Passionfruit Ginger Cheesecake — 56
- Pastry Apples with Cinnamon Custard — 90

PASTRY
- Apple Tarte Tatin — 91
- Apricot Almond Pithivier — 82
- Boysenberry Fillo Flan — 87
- Custard Apple and Passionfruit Flan — 15
- Gateau Saint Honore with Raspberry Cream — 82
- Golden Carrot Flan — 84
- Ice Cream Puffs with Tamarillo Sauce — 80
- Leaf Vol au Vents with Mango Cream — 88
- Orange Glazed Cherry Turnovers — 90
- Pastry Apples with Cinnamon Custard — 90
- Pear and Hazelnut Tart — 82
- Pecan Ganache Tart — 89
- Strawberry Glazed Yogurt Tartlets — 86
- Strawberry Rhubarb Pie — 84
- Tamarillo Almond Tartlets — 85
- Tangerine Paris-Brest — 80

- Peach Fool with Coconut Wafers, Spiced — 10
- Peach Tortoni — 44
- Peaches, Macaroon — 103
- Peachy Champagne Jelly — 3
- Peachy Ice Cream Swans — 49
- Pear and Hazelnut Tart — 82
- Pear Fritters, Toffee — 92
- Pear Ice Cream with Poached Pears, Lime and — 37
- Pears with Orange Liqueur Sauce, Poached — 104
- Pecan Dumplings in Honey Syrup — 102
- Pecan Ganache Tart — 89
- Pecan Pumpkin Cake with Cinnamon Cream — 66
- Pie, Strawberry Rhubarb — 84
- Pina Colada Mousse — 30
- Pineapple Self-Saucing Pudding — 118
- Pithivier, Apricot Almond — 82
- Plum Cheesecake with Toffee — 59
- Plum Clafouti — 104
- Plum Terrine with Sabayon Cream — 13
- Poached Pears with Orange Liqueur Sauce — 104

PUDDINGS, COLD
- Summer Fruit — 14

PUDDINGS, HOT
- Black Forest Upside-Down — 115
- Chocolate Chip — 114
- Chocolate Bread with Brandy Cream — 109
- Coffee and Hazelnut — 109
- Spicy Fig and Ginger — 113
- Steamed Pumpkin and Maple — 111
- Tangelo Syrup — 106

PUDDINGS, SELF-SAUCING
- Coffee Fudge — 118
- Ginger and Orange — 118
- Hazelnut Butterscotch — 120
- Lemon Passionfruit Delicious — 117
- Pineapple — 118

- Puffs with Tamarillo Sauce, Ice Cream — 80
- Pumpkin and Hazelnut Mousse, Spicy — 34
- Pumpkin and Maple Ice Cream — 39
- Pumpkin and Maple Pudding, Steamed — 111
- Pumpkin Cake with Cinnamon Cream, Pecan — 66

- Quick Caramel Sauce — 121

R

- Ravioli, Sweet Fried — 103
- Rhubarb and Apple Cobbler — 102
- Rhubarb Pie, Strawberry — 84
- Ricotta Chocolate Cake, Layered — 64
- Rocky Road Sauce — 122
- Rosewater Souffles — 33
- Roulade with Cherry Cream, Coconut — 66
- Rum Cheesecake, Chocolate — 60
- Rum Moulds, Butterscotch — 45
- Rum Sauce, Apricot and — 121

S

- Savarin with Cumquats, Coconut — 105

SAUCES
- Apricot and Rum — 121
- Melba — 122
- Mocha Liqueur — 122
- Passionfruit Mint — 124
- Quick Caramel — 121
- Rocky Road — 122

- Semolina Fritters with Almond Liqueur Syrup — 94

SORBETS
- Layered Pink Terrine — 47
- Lime and Mint — 36

SOUFFLES, COLD
- Caramel with Walnut Praline — 29
- Creamy Marsala — 31
- Mango with Chocolate Collars — 33
- Rosewater — 33

SOUFFLES, HOT
- Chocolate Liqueur — 100
- Coffee with Pecan Praline Cream — 96
- Fresh Apple — 96
- Ginger — 99
- Orange Liqueur with Macerated Fruits — 99
- Tamarillo Honey — 97
- Tangy Lemon — 100

- Sour Cream Cheesecake, Baked Lemon — 56
- Spiced Peach Fool with Coconut Wafers — 10
- Spicy Date Fritters with Lemon Sauce — 95
- Spicy Fig and Ginger Pudding — 113
- Spicy Pumpkin and Hazelnut Mousse — 34
- Steamed Pumpkin and Maple Pudding — 111
- Strawberry Bombe, Marbled — 54
- Strawberry Glazed Yogurt Tartlets — 86
- Strawberry Mousse with Tropical Sauce — 26
- Strawberry Parfait — 42
- Strawberry Rhubarb Pie — 84
- Summer Fruit Pudding — 14
- Sweet Fried Ravioli — 103
- Syllabub, Cumquat — 17

T

- Tamarillo Almond Tartlets — 85
- Tamarillo Honey Souffles — 97
- Tangelo Syrup Pudding — 106
- Tangerine Brioche with Creme Anglaise — 110
- Tangerine Jelly, Fresh — 4
- Tangerine Meringue Cups — 52
- Tangerine Paris-Brest — 80
- Tangy Lemon Souffle — 100
- Tart, Pear and Hazelnut — 82
- Tart, Pecan Ganache — 89
- Tarte Tatin, Apple — 91
- Tartlets, Strawberry Glazed Yogurt — 86
- Tartlets, Tamarillo Almond — 85

TERRINES
- Layered Pink Sorbet — 47
- Meringue with Chocolate Sauce — 56
- Plum with Sabayon Cream — 13

- Toffee Lattice with Fresh Fruit — 24
- Toffee Pear Fritters — 92
- Tortoni, Peach — 44
- Trifle, Brandied Apricot — 71
- Tropical Crepes Flambe — 79
- Tuiles with Blueberry Liqueur Cream — 6
- Tuiles, Macadamia with Cardamom Ice Cream — 40
- Turnovers, Orange Glazed Cherry — 90

V–Y

- Vol au Vents with Mango Cream, Leaf — 88
- Waffles with Pecan Sauce, Ginger — 116
- Walnut Gingerbread Ice Cream — 40
- Yogurt, Custard Apple Coconut — 23